An APPEAL to
HEAVEN

A Cry for Divine Justice

Dr. John D. Diamond

An Appeal to Heaven
A Cry for Divine Justice
by Dr. John D. Diamond

Printed in the United States of America.

ISBN 9781498495790

www.xulonpress.com

Table of Contents

"The longer I live, the more I am convinced that God governs in the affairs of man, and that if the American nation could not start without His assistance, its restoration and salvation will fail without Him also."

~ Dr. John D. Diamond

History is full of examples of a particular people being subjected to racial, political, economic, moral, and even religious injustice. Injustice results when the government fails to protect the God-given rights of a particular group, or worse yet, when the government itself creates policies, laws and rulings that create the social injustice. Too often, the oppressed feel that their only recourse is to allow themselves to suffer under the injustice, or just as wrong, to take the law into their own hands in order to end the injustice. However, leaders throughout history who have had a biblical world view, understand that neither of these positions ever lead to the end of injustice. What then is there left to do?

There is a very powerful biblical option, and although it often times get lost to history, it always resurfaces when it is needed once again. The Children of Israel understood it. The American Founding Fathers understood it. The abolitionists understood it. Rev. Martin Luther King understood it. As the American people are once again being subjected to racial, political, economic, moral, and even religious injustice, it is once again time to resurrect this long forgotten principle. It is simply called, *An Appeal to Heaven: A Cry for Divine Justice.*

Acknowledgements

To the men and women of the Christian and Missionary Alliance– Without your prayers and support, this project would not be possible. Thank you.

To the team at Kafferlin Strategies – Your strategic planning, work, and wise counsel has guided us through every step of the process. Thank you.

To the team at Rosie Marketing – Your marketing advice and video services have helped to shape the project from start to finish. Thank you.

Finally, to my beautiful wife, Terri, and my sons Nicholas, Matthew, Jason and Daniel – I cannot imagine for a minute my life without all of you at my side. With you all, I am complete.

Dedication

To the King of kings, Lord of lords and Judge of judges; whose Divine Law and Sovereign Rule is superior in obligation to any other, is binding over the entire globe, in all countries, and at all times; who still governs in the affairs of men and is preparing mankind to rule and reign with Him now and in the age to come.

Prayer

Vindicate us Lord, and plead our cause against an ungodly nation. Get justice for us from our adversaries. Deliver us from deceitful and unjust men. Cause them to fall into the pit that they have dug for the righteous. Grant to Your servants that we may speak Your word in all boldness. Give us the nations for our inheritance, and the ends of the earth for our possession.

A Phrase, a Symbol, a Prayer

What is the "Appeal to Heaven?"

"Have we now forgotten that powerful friend? Or do we imagine that we no longer need His assistance? I have lived, Sir, a long time, and the longer I live, the more convincing proofs I see of this truth–that God Governs in the affairs of men. And if a sparrow cannot fall to the ground without his notice, is it probable that an empire can rise without his aid?" [1]

~ Benjamin Franklin

As individuals, we all have some particular cause that we are passionate about. Whether we are passionate about finding a cure for autism or breast cancer, or simply raising awareness on things like environmental issues, Americans have proven that we are willing to sacrifice both time and money to serve as individual advocates and ambassadors for these types of awareness campaigns. It is built into mankind to want to become a part of something much bigger than ourselves and to be able to look back upon our lives and say we somehow contributed to leaving behind a better world for our children, and our children's children. All of us want to look back on our existence and say: "My life had purpose!" This is what gave rise to our "Appeal to Heaven" Campaign.

---

[1] Benjamin Franklin, "Constitutional Convention Address On Prayer" (Speech, Philadelphia, PA, June 28, 1787), America Rhetoric, http://www.americanrhetoric. com/speeches/benfranklin.htm

The "Appeal to Heaven" campaign is the phrase, symbol and prayer that Peacemakers Outreach has established for a new civil rights movement. The purpose is to first, raise awareness about our God-given and constitutionally protected rights, and then institute measures that will restore them. Our aim is to reestablish a biblical understanding of authority and the divine order of the universe, as well as the relationship between that divine order and civil government. Simply put, an "Appeal to Heaven" is a *very specific prayer* imploring the assistance of Heaven (God) to intervene and deliver His people from the hands of their oppressors when they find themselves subjected to oppression, bondage, slavery or tyranny. It is a call for God to step in as an arbitrator and execute divine justice on behalf of His people!

While the phrase "Appeal to Heaven" is not specifically used in scripture, the principle is taught repeatedly. Its application has been proven both biblically and historically to be the *only effective strategy* for the deliverance of those who are being oppressed by a more powerful adversary, whether physical, spiritual or both.

The Greek word for *appeal* (epikaleomai) means: "to invoke someone for aid." This Greek word can also be translated as "to call upon," as can be seen in Roman 10:13: "For whosoever *shall call upon* (epikaleomai) the name of the Lord shall be saved." Therefore, the word carries the idea of calling upon or appealing to a higher authority for assistance. For example, when the high priest and the chief men of the Jews conspired to kill the apostle Paul, he "appealed" unto Caesar: "*Then Festus, when he had conferred with the council, answered, 'You have appealed* (epikaleomai) *to Caesar? To Caesar you shall go!'*" (Acts 25:12).

The divine principle of the "Appeal to Heaven" was taught by our LORD Jesus Christ Himself in the parable of the persistent widow:

> Then He spoke a parable to them, that men always ought to pray and not lose heart, saying: "There was in a certain city a judge who did not fear God nor regard man. Now there was a widow in that city; and she came to him, saying, 'Get justice for me from my adversary.' And he would not for a while; but

afterward he said within himself, 'Though I do not fear God nor regard man, yet because this widow troubles me I will avenge her, lest by her continual coming she weary me.'" Then the Lord said, "Hear what the unjust judge said. And shall God not avenge His own elect who cry out day and night to Him, though He bears long with them? I tell you that He will avenge them speedily. Nevertheless, when the Son of Man comes, will He really find faith on the earth?"

~ Luke 18:1-8

The widow's plea to "get justice for me from my adversary" was her way of taking a case to court in the form of a lawsuit and pleading for her rights to be restored and for the oppression to end. The "Appeal to Heaven," therefore, is an act of faith in which God's people petition or "call upon God" to interpose; that is, to serve as the final and highest arbitrator or mediator between two conflicting parties. As American citizens, we once again find ourselves subjected to a small group of deceitful and unjust men who have plotted a vain thing. *They have replaced the LORD as the Supreme King, Lawgiver and Judge and have used the unlawful power of the government* (also known as tyranny) *to force people of faith to obey their unjust mandates.*

For years, legal teams have appealed these unjust rulings to the highest court in the land, but to no avail. In every stage of these oppressions, we have patiently and humbly petitioned for that body to address our grievances, but our petitions have been answered only by repeated injury and further usurpations.

As we will see, an "Appeal to Heaven" is *the only* historically effective and proven strategy that can be used by an oppressed people in order to be freed from the adversary or oppressors when all other strategies have failed. As Americans, we need to ask ourselves, once again, the age old question Benjamin Franklin asked the committee at the constitutional convention: "Have we now [as Americans] forgotten that powerful friend? Or do we imagine that we no longer need His assistance?"

The longer I live, the more I am convinced that God governs in the affairs of man, and that if the American nation could not start without His assistance, its restoration and salvation will fail without Him also.

~ Dr. John D. Diamond
Erie, Pennsylvania

The Straw that Broke the Camel's Back

Is America in a Downward Cycle?

"Men fight for liberty and win it with hard knocks. Their children, brought up easy, let it slip away again, poor fools. And their grand-children are once more slaves."[2]

~ D.H. Lawrence

S ecular and biblical scholars have both noticed a pattern throughout human history. All of the world's greatest civilizations have started in some type of bondage, either physical, spiritual, or in most cases, both. This truth becomes apparent through a study of antiquity from a secular and biblical worldview. Either way, and no matter the presuppositions of the scholar, the facts are the same and speak for themselves.

Scottish historian Alexander Fraser Tyler, Professor of Universal History and Greek and Roman Antiquities, is said to have written:

A democracy cannot exist as a permanent form of government. It can only exist until the voters discover

---

[2] David Herbert Lawrence, "Liberty's Old Old Story" in *The Complete Poems of David Herbert Lawrence*, edited by Vivian De Sola Pinto and F Warren Roberts (Hertfordshire: Wordsworth Editions Limited, 1994), 535.

that they can vote themselves largesse [benefits] from the public treasury. From that moment on, the majority always votes for the candidates promising the most benefits from the public treasury with the result that a democracy always collapses over lousy fiscal policy, always followed by a dictatorship. The average of the world's great civilizations before they decline has been 200 years. These nations have progressed in this sequence: From bondage to spiritual faith; from faith to great courage; from courage to liberty; from liberty to abundance; from abundance to selfishness; from selfishness to complacency; from complacency to apathy; from apathy to dependency; from dependency back again to bondage.[3]

In America, we have been led to believe that our system of government is stable and will endure forever, but history shows otherwise. We also tend to believe that America is the first and only country, at this point in history, to institute "democracy" as its form of government. However, Athens was also a democracy, and it too failed. Using history as our guide, we can listen to what many of our Founding Fathers had to say about the history of democracies.

John Adams wrote, "Remember, Democracy never lasts long. It soon wastes, exhausts, and murders itself. There never was a democracy yet that did not commit suicide."[4] Benjamin Rush, who signed the Declaration of Independence, said, "A simple democracy... is one of the greatest of evils."[5] Noah Webster is also quoted as saying, "In democracy... there are common tumults and disorders... Therefore, a pure democracy is generally a very bad government. It is often

---

[3] Elmer T Peterson, "This Is The Hard Core Of Freedom," *The Daily Oklahoman*, 12A, December 9, 1951.

[4] John Adams, *John Adams To John Taylor December 17, 1814*, Letter, From: National Archives, http://founders.archives.gov/documents/Adams/99-02-02-6371

[5] Benjamin Rush, *Benjamin Rush to John Adams July 21, 1789,* Letter, From: The Founders' Constitution, http://press-pubs.uchicago.edu/founders/documents/v1ch4s30.html

the most tyrannical government on earth."[6] John Quincy Adams said: "The experience of all former ages has shown that of all human governments, democracy was the most unstable, fluctuating, and short lived." In Federalist No. 10, James Madison wrote, "Democracies... have, in general, been as short in their lives as they have been violent in their deaths."[7]

Upon leaving one of the many sessions of the Constitutional Convention held in Philadelphia in 1787, Benjamin Franklin, who was one of the delegates, was asked what type of government they had created for America. "A Republic, if you can keep it,"[8] was his reply.

In a republic, ideally both the government and its citizens are guided and governed by a set of higher laws. This is what we call the *Doctrine of Higher Authority*. In a democracy, however, the nation is governed by a sort of mob mentality, and whatever the majority wants or votes for becomes the law. However, what if the majority votes to take your money, or your house or your children? There is nothing to stop them from getting their way. In contrast, government under a constitutional republic recognizes higher law, and protects a person's money, property and children from the mob. It is for this reason that mob rule degenerates, and has historically been the worst type of government. Unless the majority of people, as a collective group, is restrained by a higher sense of right and wrong, democracy will fail

When seeking to create the American system of Government, our Founding Fathers had a clean slate to work with. They understood that God had already given mankind a perfect moral code when he

---

[6] Noah Webster, *The American Spelling Book: Containing an Easy Standard of Pronunciation: Being the First Part of a Grammatical Institute of the English Language, To Which is Added, an Appendix, Containing a Moral Catechism and a Federal Catechism, Edited by* Isaiah Thomas and Ebenezer T. Andrews (Boston: 1801), pp. 103-104.

[7] James Madison, *Federalist No. 10,* Essay, November 22, 1787, Source: Teaching America History, http://teachingamericanhistory.org/library/document/federalist-no-10/

[8] Richard R. Beeman, "Perspectives On The Constitution: A Republic, If You Can Keep It," National Constitution Center, http://constitutioncenter.org/learn/educational-resources/historical-documents/perspectives-on-the-constitution-a-republic-if-you-can-keep-it

led the Israelites out of Egypt.[9] Yet, for the last 4000 years, man, in his arrogance, has been trying to change and fix what was never broken.. Under the divinely directed system of government, Israel was established as a kind of a republican structure of government – and one that recognized higher law; a nation in which government, culture and society are shaped and formed on a set of higher laws that apply to all people equally. This system of government protected the rights of people, and their property, from the elected or appointed officials. They had no king or congress, only a series of judges and elders who would defer to God's law in order to determine what was both legal and moral. This type of biblically-based constitutional republic is what the Founders were trying to recreate. They were not merely trying to replace the British monarchy with the mob rule, democratic style. Rather, they desired to replace a tyrannical and despotic king with a wise and benevolent ruler known as the King of Heaven and the Lord of Hosts. This is the position that was advocated by Thomas Paine in his Revolutionary War Handbook, *Common Sense*.

> Near three thousand years passed away from the Mosaic account of the creation, till the Jews under a national delusion requested a king. Till then their form of government (except in extraordinary cases, where the Almighty interposed) was a kind of republic administered by a judge and the elders of the tribes. Kings they had none, and it was held sinful to acknowledge any being under that title but the Lord of Hosts. And when a man seriously reflects on the idolatrous homage which is paid to the persons of kings, he need not wonder that the Almighty, ever jealous of his honour, should disapprove of a form of

---

[9] That is, God gave the perfect moral code to ancient Israel, which remains operative for all people and for all time. It is not the contention of this author that the civil and ceremonial laws of ancient Israel are, or need be, mandatory and normative today.

government which so impiously invades the prerogative of heaven.[10]

After God freed the Israelites from Egyptian bondage, He warned them of a nation's inclination to fall into a downward cycle. Generally, the cycle follows these steps:

Peace and prosperity - the promises of blessing (Deut 28:1-14)

Abundance (Deut 8:11-14)[3]

Apathy and compromise (Deut 8:11-17)

Rebellion (humanism) and paganism (Judges 3:7)

Famine, war, plagues and slavery (Judges 3:8)

Confession and repentance - the people recognize their need for God (Judges 3:9)

God hears their "Appeal to Heaven" and saves and restores their nation (Judges 3:9-10)

The American Republic was based upon a proper understanding of the *Doctrine of Higher Authority* (found in Romans 13) and Thomas Jefferson's "laws of nature and nature's God," which are showcased in the Declaration of Independence. Unfortunately, the

---

[10] Thomas Paine, *Common Sense,* Essay, January 9, 1776, Source: Bill of Rights Institute, https://billofrightsinstitute.org/founding-documents/primary-source-documents/common-sense/

system of government (an American Republic) that was created by our Founding Fathers was gradually unrooted from her principled founding, and consequently, we should expect our future to mimic a historical pattern.

The biblical-historical cycle of the nation of Israel virtually mirrors the secular cycle. The biblical model shows the cause, while the secular model shows the effect.[11] Therefore, the cycle, as explained by Tyler, can also be charted as follows:

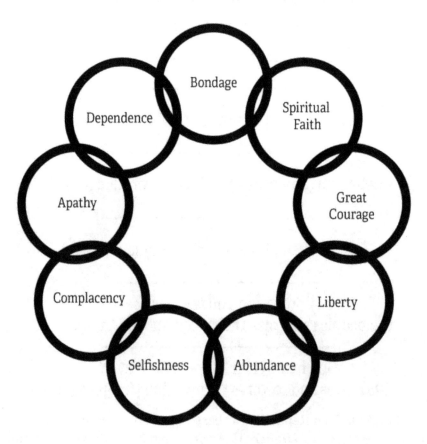

It is only when God raises up faithful and courageous leaders who appeal to Heaven for guidance in order to end oppression that a nation once again can enjoy a period of peace and prosperity. Unfortunately,

---

[11] Deut 8:11-14 NKJV

this historical cycle is presently repeating itself in America as we go from bondage to freedom, from freedom to prosperity, and from prosperity back to bondage.

History has all but proven that government, or those in power, increasingly and incrementally seek to control and subjugate every area of life until the populace is treated more like slaves than citizens. *This is what our Founding Fathers called Tyranny.* For many years, an apathetic populace will turn a blind eye to these abuses and incremental usurpations of power until they become so unbearable that the people rise up and say: "Enough!" For many years, the citizenry will petition their leaders for the restoration of their rights and liberties until they realize their government has no intention of reversing its institutional control over them. Eventually, something will cause a "straw that breaks the camel's back" reaction. This generally results in an armed conflict in which the people seek to free themselves from oppressive government control. This is, of course, the story of our American nation. The Declaration of Independence states:

> All experience hath shewn, that mankind are more disposed to suffer, while evils are sufferable, than to right themselves by abolishing the forms to which they are accustomed. But when a long train of abuses and usurpations, pursuing invariably the same Object evinces a design to reduce them under absolute Despotism, it is their right, it is their duty, to throw off such Government, and to provide new Guards for their future security.[12]

Where, then, does present-day America fit into this cycle? Americans today are becoming increasingly aware that their own federal government more closely resembles the tyrannical empire they broke away from than it does the Constitutional Republic that was created following the Revolutionary War. In a report published May 1, 2013 by Fairleigh Dickinson University, it was found that

---

[12] Thomas Jefferson, *The Declaration of Independence,* Essay, July 4th, 1776, http://teachingamericanhistory.org/library/document/declaration-of-independence/

a sizeable portion of Americans surveyed believe that: "In the next few years, an armed revolution might be necessary in order to protect our liberties...."[13]

Why would a growing number of Americans think that an armed revolution against their own government may be necessary? Why are an alarmingly high number of Americans taking such a pessimistic, and even fatalistic, view of our future as a nation?

Even now, Christian churches, parachurch organizations, and even Christian owned businesses are beginning to feel the "chains" of oppressive government control. The Supreme Court has overstepped both its moral and constitutional authority and has established itself as the governing oligarchy. Unaccountable justices are imposing secular religion with a new and un-American standard of morality upon the people. The federal court system now demands acceptance and tolerance of everybody and everything—except expressions of religious faith and the Right of Conscience.

Make no mistake about it. This cannot be sustained. A revolution is coming. It may come upon us quickly or it may be decades away. It may take the form of war, or it could be cultural. Nevertheless, this sentiment has been festering below the surface for over a generation. In a report presented to the United States Senate in May, 1966, Robert F. Kennedy is quoted as saying: "A revolution is coming – a revolution which will be peaceful if we are wise enough; compassionate if we care enough; successful if we are fortunate enough – but a revolution which is coming whether we will it or not. *We can affect its character; we cannot alter its inevitability*."[14]

His words were truer than he realized. The question is whether this eventual and inevitable revolution will be led by violent and unprincipled men, resulting in an armed and bloody conflict, or whether it will be a peaceful revolution led by Peacemakers, who are guided by divine principles and aided by Heaven itself.

---

[13] Dan Cassino and Krista Jenkina, "Beliefs About Sandy Hook Cover-Up, Coming Revolution Underline Divide On Gun Control," Fairleigh Dickinson University, May 1, 2013, http://www.fdu.edu/newspubs/publicmind/2013/guncontrol/final.pdf

[14] Robert F. Kennedy, "Report to the United States Senate on his trip to Latin America and the Alliance for Progress," (Speech: Washington, DC, May 9, 1966)

We advocate the latter. But what will it take to end the tyranny and restore our American Constitutional Republic? History has the answers. As our Founding Fathers taught us, it will take an "Appeal to Heaven":

> We, therefore, the Representatives of the United States of America... *appealing to the Supreme Judge of the world* for the [righteousness] of our intentions, do, in the Name, and by Authority of the good People of these Colonies, solemnly publish and declare, that these United Colonies are, and of Right ought to be Free and Independent States. And for the support of this Declaration, with a firm reliance on the protection of divine Providence, we mutually pledge to each other our Lives, our Fortunes and our sacred Honor.[15]

It is for this reason that we are "Appealing to Heaven" for the launch of a new civil rights movement.

---

[15] Thomas Jefferson, *The Declaration of Independence,* Essay, July 4th, 1776, http://teachingamericanhistory.org/library/document/declaration-of-independence/

Rebuking the Oppressors

Do We Need Another Civil Rights Movement?

*"Freedom is never more than one generation away
from extinction. We didn't pass it to our children in
the bloodstream. It must be fought for, protected, and
handed on for them to do the same, or one day we will
spend our sunset years telling our children and our
children's children what it was once like in the United
States where men were free."*[16]

~ Ronald Reagan

Tyranny. Despotism. Oligarchy. Usurpation. Ask most Americans to define these terms and use them in a sentence, and you would be surprised how many are unable to do so. These terms have essentially been stricken from the American vocabulary and educational system, yet they were used quite frequently by our Founding Fathers. Most Americans do not see any need for a new civil rights movement because they do not understand what these terms mean. They do not know what God, throughout scripture, has said about the eternal struggle between good and evil and the role His people are to play in this spiritual conflict. I have found, however, that when these terms and

---

[16] Ronald Reagan, "A Foot In The Door" (Speech: Illinois, May 9, 1961), Reagan Foundation, http://reagan.convio.net/site/DocServer/ ReaganMomentsFeb_-_1__-_A_Foot_InThe_Door_5.9.6.pdf?docID=581

definitions are reintroduced, defined, and clarified, the need for such a movement is seen as compelling, necessary, and even as our duty to the Supreme Ruler of the universe.

British historian Lord Acton was once quoted as saying, "Power tends to corrupt; absolute power corrupts absolutely."[17] This lust for power has historically led to many abuses by the ruling class over their subjects and fellow citizens. In his Farewell Address on September 19, 1796, George Washington warned of the tendency of the human heart to lust for, and abuse, government power:

It is important, likewise, that the habits of thinking in a free Country should *inspire caution in those entrusted with its (government) administration*, to confine themselves within their respective Constitutional spheres; avoiding in the exercise of the Powers of one department to encroach upon another. The spirit of encroachment tends to consolidate the powers of all the departments in one, and thus to create whatever the form of government, a real despotism. *A just estimate of that love of power, and proneness to abuse it, which predominates in the human heart is sufficient to satisfy us of the truth of this position.*[18]

Despotism is defined as: "Absolute power; authority unlimited and uncontrolled by men, constitution or laws."[19] Despotism results from a corruption of power in which civil authorities (our fellow man) refuse to be controlled by either constitutions or laws and seek to control and subjugate every area of life. Simply put, despotism is a reference to out-of-control government officials who have been so corrupted by power that they forget they are mere men; they begin to think they are the Supreme Rulers of the universe.

In order to generate support for a new civil rights movement, it will first be necessary both to articulate the present need for such a movement and to provide a biblical justification for the proposed course of action. A simple illustration would be helpful. Consider the story of a

---

[17] "Lord Acton Quote Archive," Acton Institute, 2016, http://www.acton.org/research/lord-acton-quote-archive

[18] George Washington, *Farewell Address*," Essay, September 19, 1796, Teaching American History, http://teachingamericanhistory.org/library/document/farewell-address

[19] *Webster's 1828 English Dictionary*, s.v. "Despotism," http://sorabji.com/1828/words/d/despotism.html

young boy who faces daily intimidation on his way to school; a bully insists the child surrender his milk money or face physical retaliation.

A bully may be classified as a person who is habitually cruel to those who are weaker in order to impose his will by force, intimidation or threats. As a parent, our first response may be to let the child handle the situation and be strong. A parent may tell him to stand up to the bully. Otherwise, this type of behavior will just continue. However, what if your child is just 6 years old and the bully is 17? In this scenario, your child would be too weak and powerless to defend himself. Now, as a father or mother, if your child appealed to you for help in order to stop bullying, would you turn him away, or would you take measures to ensure that this behavior does not continue? As a parent, would you not intervene in order to stop this type of oppressive and even illegal behavior?

How much more, then, would our Heavenly Father step in when we Appeal to Heaven for assistance? Our Heavenly Father hates when people oppress one another. Any abuse or injustice in any society is purely artificial, man-made and not authorized by the LORD. Unfortunately, mankind has proven to have an innate desire within himself to control, dominate and oppress his fellow man, especially those individuals who are too weak and powerless to defend themselves.

In the Old Testament, whenever the man of the house passed away, it was the tendency of wicked and unjust men to oppress and otherwise take advantage of his widow and children because they were left with no one to defend them. For this reason, the LORD had to issue a command for men *not* to treat their fellow man in this manner. As a matter of fact, God calls this type of treatment evil. "Do not oppress the widow or the fatherless, the alien or the poor. Let none of you plan evil in his heart against his brother."[20]

Scripture teaches that our Heavenly Father not only sees such wickedness and oppression, but He will also intervene in the lives of the petitioner and deal with the wicked. "The LORD watches over the strangers; He relieves the fatherless and widow; but the way of the

---

[20] Zech 7:10 NKJV

wicked He turns upside down."[21] Scripture also teaches, "The LORD executes righteousness and justice for all who are oppressed."[22]

Jesus spoke about the gentile's political leaders (rulers) and their unrighteous tendency to oppress or tyrannize their fellow man: "You know that the rulers of the Gentiles lord it over them, and those who are great *exercise authority* over them."[23] The phrase "exercise authority" means "to control or to subjugate." This is the very definition of tyranny. The Amplified Bible translates it in this way: "And Jesus called them to Him and said, you know that the rulers of the Gentiles lord it over them, and their great men hold them in subjection [tyrannizing over them]."[24]

As God's people, we are forbidden from oppressing the weak and powerless, but we are also not to sit by quietly and idly while these abuses are taking place. We are commanded to *rebuke* those that are committing such atrocities: "Wash yourselves, make yourselves clean; Put away the evil of your doings from before My eyes. Cease to do evil, Learn to do good; Seek justice, *Rebuke the oppressor; Defend the fatherless, Plead for the widow.*"[25]

God's people are commanded to stand up and defend those who are too weak politically, socially or economically to defend themselves against those who are using their political positions of power and authority to oppress their fellow man. This duty to rebuke the oppressors even extends to our political leaders. Jesus was telling his disciples that because the Gentiles did not know God or His ways, they did not understand God's directives in this area and therefore, must be admonished by those who did have this knowledge.[26] Rebuking the oppressors must be done by those who understand from scripture that we are all God's creation, and that it is contrary to the will of God for the rich and powerful to suppress, control or subjugate the weak and powerless.

---

[21] Ps 146:9 NKJV

[22] Ps 103:6 NKJV

[23] Matt 20:25 NKJV

[24] Matt 20:25 AMP

[25] Isa 1:16-17 NKJV

[26] Romans 2:14, Gal 4:8, 1 Thess 4:5 NKJV

> Listen, my beloved brethren: Has God not chosen the poor of this world to be rich in faith and heirs of the kingdom which He promised to those who love Him? But you have dishonored the poor man. Do not the rich oppress you and drag you into the courts? Do they not blaspheme that noble name by which you are called?[27]

In a practical sense, this rebuke can only occur when a person or a group of people, who are in possession of both faith and courage, rise up and declare to the powerful oppressors: "Just because you are rich or more powerful does not give you the divine right to treat people who are weaker than you in this way!" There is no group of people with a greater capacity—or the faith, courage and the divine authority—to take the lead in this endeavor than the church of Jesus Christ.

Unfortunately, the Christian church has lost its place and seems to have abdicated both its political and its divine authority. This "divine authority" was given by God the Father to His Son Jesus Christ, who in turn gave it to the church.[28] This is what it means to be the "salt" and the "light."[29] Until now, we in the church have lost the idea that we have been given this authority to "exhort, and rebuke with all authority," or have been too timid, reluctant or complacent to operate by this authority.[30]

Isn't the church's primary responsibility to tell *every soul* to repent when they violate the doctrine of higher authority, the rules of eternal justice, and to scold those who trifle with the moral law of God? Since when did government officials become exempt from this? If the Christian church will not rebuke the civil leaders and remind them that they are not at the top of the universal chain-of-command, then who will?

Those who say that Christians should not be involved in rebuking political leaders when they defy the laws of God must explain the following biblical accounts. In every case, God made sure that his divine will was known. These government leaders refused to comply, and God had to send a prophet to rebuke them.

---

[27] James 2:5-7 NKJV

[28] Matt 28:18 NKJV

[29] Matt 5:13-16 NKJV

[30] Titus 2:15 NKJV

Moses rebuking Pharaoh, an example of a government leader being rebuked–Afterward Moses and Aaron went in and told Pharaoh, *"Thus says the LORD God of Israel: 'Let My people go, that they may hold a feast to Me in the wilderness.' And Pharaoh said, 'Who is the LORD, that I should obey His voice to let Israel go? I do not know the LORD, nor will I let Israel go.'"*[31]

Elijah rebuking King Ahab, an example of a government leader being rebuked – *"Then Elijah said, 'As the LORD of hosts lives, before whom I stand, I will surely present myself to him today.' So Obadiah went to meet Ahab, and told him; and Ahab went to meet Elijah. Then it happened, when Ahab saw Elijah that Ahab said to him, 'Is that you, O troubler of Israel?' And he answered, 'I have not troubled Israel, but you and your father's house have, in that you have forsaken the commandments of the LORD and have followed the Baals.'"*[32]

John the Baptist rebuking King Herod, is an example of a government leader being rebuked – *"But when Herod heard, he said, 'This is John, whom I beheaded; he has been raised from the dead!' For Herod himself had sent and laid hold of John, and bound him in prison for the sake of Herodias, his brother Philip's wife; for he had married her. Because John had said to Herod, 'It is not lawful for you to have your brother's wife.'"*[33]

Jesus rebuking the Sadducees and Pharisees, and example of government leaders being rebuked– One of the chief objections from those who think the church should not be involved in politics is that "Jesus never got involved in politics!" This is fundamentally untrue. These statements come from a biblical ignorance of the make-up of the Jewish political system.

The Jews did not have a congress (i.e. lawmakers) as we do in America today. God had already given the heart of Jewish law (civil,

---

[31] Ex 5:1-2 NKJV

[32] 1 Kings 18:15-19 NKJV

[33] Mark 6:16-18 NKJV

moral and ceremonial) through the hand of Moses. Moreover, in Jewish society, any new laws had to be consistent with this original foundation; they could not nullify the commandments delivered through Moses or obscure the original intent of the Ten Commandments—the spirit of the laws, which as Jesus said, is to love God and love our neighbor. Jesus' strongest rebukes were against lawyers and political and religious leaders.[34]

It was in fact the Pharisees that were given the authority to sit in Moses' seat.[35] They were the judges and elders who would defer to God's law in order to determine what was both legal and moral in Jewish society. However, like the judges of old, they were supposed to be acting under a *delegated authority*. Unfortunately, the corruption of this political power took its toll on these leaders like all others. Jesus' biggest confrontations and rebukes were leveled at these three groups (Sadducees, Pharisees and Lawyers) because they were using their political power and distorted interpretations of the divine law to enslave the Jewish people under a plethora of traditions, legislation, and ungodly interpretations of the law.[36]

This was handled by an assembly or high council known as the Sanhedrin, which was created during the time of Moses and made up of seventy elders (priests, scribes, lawyers), led by the High Priest.[37] It was the responsibility of this political and judicial council or assembly to interpret and enforce all aspects of the Mosaic Law, which consisted of not only sacrificial and ceremonial law, but also the or governmental civil laws.

At the time of Christ, the post of High Priest was occupied by Caiaphas, and during the time of Paul, it was occupied by Ananias. During the Roman occupation of Israel, both were political appointments made by Rome. The American governmental body most resembling the Sanhedrin would be the U.S. Supreme Court, with the Chief Priest serving as president or Chief Justice of this "high council."

---

[34] Matt 23, Luke 11 NKJV

[35] Matt 23:2 NKJV

[36] Matt 23:1-36 NKJV

[37] Num 11:16-17, Ex 24:1-2 NKJV

All of the members of the Sanhedrin belonged primarily to one of two dominate political parties: The Sadducees and the Pharisees. These two groups were essentially political-religious groups that were somewhat like today's political parties. A person could be a scribe or a lawyer by profession and a member of the Pharisees' party.[38]

During the time of Christ, the Sanhedrin was dominated by a Pharisee majority with a Sadducee (Caiaphas) acting as High Priest. These two groups despised one another except when their political power was threatened.[39] Then they were seen teaming up against Jesus in order to test and discredit Him.[40] And like the U.S. government today, the Sanhedrin's unrighteous interpretations of the law tended to cause oppression, rather than protect the people from government oppression.

Similarly, it is rather ironic that the Federal government has a website titled stopbullying.gov, defining bullying as *"An Imbalance of Power: Kids who bully use their power—such as physical strength, access to embarrassing information, or popularity—to control or harm others."*[41] What happens when these bullies grow up and seek to use the power of government and media to control the lives of the American people though these same tactics? The only difference between a bully and a tyrant is that the bully begins to use the power of government (police, military or the courts) to enforce his or her unlawful edicts, using force, intimidation or threats. The word "tyranny" could, therefore, be defined as "government sanctioned bullying." As we have seen from past history, the only way to combat this flagrant abuse of power and injustice is through peaceful resistance, which is accomplished by rebuking the oppressors, defying their illegal rulings and then appealing to our Heavenly Father for assistance.

---

[38] Matt 22:34-36, Acts 23:9 NKJV

[39] Acts 23:1-10 NKJV

[40] Matt 16:1 NKJV

[41] "What is Bullying?" U.S. Department of Health and Human Services, http://www.stopbullying.gov/what-is-bullying/index.html

Uncovering the God Complex

How and Why is Power Abused?

"Now when He came into the temple, the chief priests and the elders of the people confronted Him as He was teaching, and said, 'By what authority are You doing these things? And who gave You this authority?'" [42]

Matthew 21:23

One cannot truly understand and support a civil rights movement without first having a biblical understanding of the relationship between the words "power" and "authority." The word power can be defined as either "legal authority" or "physical strength."[43] In the English language, we have one word for both definitions and must use the context of the sentence to determine which definition applies. However, in the Greek language in which the New Testament is written, there are two separate and distinct words for "power." One word (*exousia*) is used for legal authority, while the other (*dunamis*) can refer to both physical and spiritual strength.

The word (*exousia*-authority) is used in scriptures such as John 19:10-11, when Pontius Pilate incorrectly assumed that he had the

---

[42] Matt 21:23 NKJV

[43] *Merriam-Webster,* s.v. "Power,: http://www.merriam-webster.com/dictionary/power

political authority to release or crucify Christ. "Then Pilate said to Him, 'Are You not speaking to me? Do You not know that I have power (*exousia*-authority) to crucify You, and power (*exousia*-authority) to release You?' Jesus answered, 'You could have no power (*exousia*-authority) at all against Me unless it had been given you from above.'"[44]

The word (*dunamis*-strength) on the other hand is used in scriptures such as 2 Cor. 12:9-10: "And He said to me, 'My grace is sufficient for you, for My strength (*dunamis*-strength) is made perfect in weakness.' Therefore, most gladly I will rather boast in my infirmities, that the power (*dunamis*-strength) of Christ may rest upon me."[45]

Jesus possessed both the *exousia* legal authority and the *dunamis* strength over unclean spirits. "And they were all amazed, and spoke among themselves, saying, 'what a word is this! For with authority (*exousia*-authority) and power (*dunamis*-strength) he commanded the unclean spirits, and they come out.'"[46]

History is full of examples in which unjust and wicked persons attempt to use physical power to force compliance from a weaker individual without the legal authority to do so. A 17-year-old bully may have the power (physical strength) to extort the milk money from your six-year-old child, but not the power (legal authority) to do so. Without the legal authority, the bully then becomes a criminal and a thief. When government officials use physical strength (i.e. the police, the army or the courts) to enforce civil penalties (fines, jail, or death) upon its citizens without the legal authority to do so, this is known as tyranny.

As a former police officer, I was what was considered a "civil authority." While operating under the authority of law, I had a tremendous amount of power granted to me. I was even permitted to enter a house without a search warrant if I believed a crime was being committed. However, the amount of my authority was limited by the law and the Constitution. For me to search a person's house arbitrarily, just because I felt like it, would have been a violation of that

---

[44] John 19:10-11 NKJV

[45] 2 Cor 12:9-10 NKJV

[46] Luke 4:36 NKJV

authority, since citizens have rights against illegal search and seizure as protected by the Fourth Amendment to the Constitution. These rights are recognized in the Constitution so as to protect the American people from the abuses of corrupt authority figures. I may have possessed the power (a gun or a battering ram) to enter your house, but I did not possess the legal or constitutional authority to do so.

Throughout history, and once granted the reins of power either by force or election, those in power have come to dominate the lives of those they are entrusted to govern. Again, as British historian, Lord Acton, explained, "Power tends to corrupt; absolute power corrupts absolutely."[47] In times past, this corruption of political power has led to many abuses by the ruling class (or those elected to government positions) over their subjects and/or fellow citizens.

One of our Founding Fathers' chief complaints against the British crown was that the British parliament insisted that they had the authority to pass any law they chose, and would then use their army to force the colonists into compliance. This type of tyranny (government sanctioned bullying) is the exact opposite of freedom and liberty. As a matter of fact, the colonists felt that this abuse of power created conditions akin to slavery. Thomas Paine articulated the feelings of the American colonists quite well in *The Crisis*, written on December 23, 1776.

> Britain, with an army to enforce her tyranny, has declared that she has a right (not only to TAX) but "to BIND us in ALL CASES WHATSOEVER" and if being bound in that manner, is not slavery, then is there not such a thing as slavery upon earth. Even the expression is impious; for so unlimited a power can belong only to God.[48]

---

[47] Lord Acton, Letter to Archbishop Mandell Creighton, April 5, 1887, Letter, Liberty Fund,
http://oll.libertyfund.org/titles/acton-acton-creighton-correspondence#lf1524_label_010

[48] Thomas Paine, *The Crisis*, Essay, December 23, 1776, Independence Hall Association, http://www.ushistory.org/paine/crisis/c-01.htm

This impious expression of power is what I call a "god-complex." A god-complex is a condition that results from an intoxication of power in which political leaders, kings, law-makers and judges begin to believe that their authority is unlimited. They begin to imagine they are the highest authority on earth and have the right to issue orders, commands, or pass laws which violate the strict parameters of their legal authority.

Allow me to share a couple of personal testimonies in order to show how this "god-complex" develops and what a person should do when confronted by it. Upon entering the U.S. Air Force at age 18, I found myself at the bottom of a very large chain-of-command. With so many individuals above me issuing lawful orders, I oftentimes found myself in what is known as a "no-win" or "catch-22" situation. A catch-22 occurs when a subordinate finds himself faced with a set of contradictory orders issued by superiors. When, for example, two sergeants of equal rank gave me a series of contradictory orders, I would call the two sergeants together and explain my dilemma. I would explain: "I have no problem respecting and honoring those in authority above me. However, unknown to the other, you have placed me in a catch-22 situation. If I obey the orders of one, I am disobeying the orders of the other. Therefore, you must get together and reach a conclusion on which order I should follow."

When two sergeants of different ranks issued me a set of contradictory orders, the situation was much easier to navigate. Even though I was faced with another catch-22 situation, I would simply obey the higher authority and disobey the lower authority. There was, in fact, no other option. This was not always received well by the sergeant of lower rank, however. When confronted by the lower-ranking sergeant as to why I disobeyed a lawful order, I would inform him that he was outranked by the lawful orders of his superior. It surprised me how often this answer did not satisfy. When the lower-ranking sergeant continued to harass me about my disobedience to his orders, I would appeal to the higher authority. I would call in the higher-ranking sergeant to act as an arbitrator between myself and my other superior. When it became clear that the lower-ranking sergeant disregarded a higher order, it often did not bode well for him because now he was the one who had forgotten or ignored his place in the chain-of-command. This is the only appropriate way in which to handle these types of situations and individuals.

Here is another similar situation. Several years ago, I was working for a very large electric utility company in Columbus, Ohio. My job was to install and maintain the electric grid under the city, which ran through a series of vaults and manholes. Being the senior union lineman at the time, I was given the task to oversee contractors hired to install electrical cables in the newly-constructed Nationwide Arena complex. My job was to give them a briefing and to ensure that all government regulations mandated by the Occupational Safety and Health Administration (OSHA) and company safety policies were being complied with. I was also tasked with authorizing entry into manholes, which are considered "confined spaces" by OSHA.

I was the company instructor for all First Aid/CPR training, as well as the instructor for all company personnel needing OSHA certification to enter a confined space. OSHA law (and our company safety manual) requires certain conditions be met before any individual is permitted to enter a confined space. They are as follows:

1. All personnel tasked with performing duties within a confined space must have attended confined-entry training.
2. All individuals must be certified in First Aid/CPR.
3. Before opening or entering a confined space, the space must first be tested to ensure the atmosphere is breathable and that no dangerous or explosive gases are present.
4. Once the manhole cover has been removed, provisions must be made to prevent personnel or bystanders from falling into the hole. A rescue device must also be present for emergency situations if carrying a full grown man up a ladder is not feasible.
5. A government document had to be signed by a qualified "entry supervisor," verifying that all the above provisions were met before allowing entry into the confined space.

Upon arriving at the jobsite, I made contact with the contract personnel. I immediately noticed they had the manhole cover off, but the hole was not barricaded in order to prevent people from falling in, risking injury. I asked the contractors if they had a manhole rescue rack. They told me they did not. I then asked if they had taken an air sample before removing the manhole cover so no dangerous or explosive gases were present. Again, they had not. I then explained that according to OSHA law, I could not permit them entry until the above requirements had been met. Not wanting to shut down the job completely, I told them I would go back into our shop and bring out all the required equipment (i.e. manhole barricade, air monitor, etc.). On the way back to our shop, I called my department head and advised him of the situation. He agreed I took the right course of action.

Then I began to think about the provisions I had taught for so many years. I soon realized that if these individuals received the required OSHA confined entry training, they would have known all of these requirements. Therefore, they had either not had the training or were willfully defying the requirements.

Returning to the jobsite, I asked if they had received the required training. They responded that they had not. I advised that according to federal law, I would not be able to sign the government document allowing entry into the confined space, which prompted them to call their supervisor. Several minutes later, their boss showed up and was irate. I advised him of the law and that if he had any further problems with my decision, he could take it up with my department head. I even offered him my cell phone to call my supervisor.

After a few minutes of conferring with my boss, he handed the phone back with a smile and said, "He said to let us in the manhole." Convinced there was a miscommunication about the situation, I got on the phone with my boss and was ordered to allow them entry into the hole. Realizing this was not a lawful order, I advised him to contact his boss for further clarification. He called me back several minutes later with the same response–his boss also said to let them in the hole.

This placed me in a no-win situation. If I were to obey the federal law, then I would be disobeying the orders of my boss. If I obeyed the order of my boss, on the other hand, I would be in defiance of federal law. Clear in my understanding of the doctrine of higher authority, I knew exactly what to do. I responded to my boss in the following manner:

Let me make this very clear to you. Neither you nor your boss has the authority to command me to violate a federal law. You are overstepping your authority by so ordering. If I sign this legal document and allow these unqualified workers entry into this confined space, I could find myself both criminally and civilly liable. Therefore, I am not allowing them entry into this confined space! You essentially have three choices before you now. 1) You can come out yourself and sign the document allowing entry into the space, thus making yourself criminally and civilly liable in the event of an accident. 2) You can send some other person out to relieve me of my duties, at which time I will advise them of their responsibility under the law. 3) You can replace the contractors with our personnel, who have been properly trained and equipped.

I went on to advise him that: "The ball is now in your court! You do whatever you need to do from this point on, but I will not comply with your orders because they are not lawful." He opted for option #3.

Historically, refusing to comply with the unlawful edicts of a higher authority is known as "manly firmness," for it requires courage to tell those in authority that you will not comply with their unjust orders. This will be explored further in the following chapter.

As you can imagine, people in authority do not like being disobeyed by their subordinates, even when the subordinate has taken the proper legal position. It should come as no surprise, then, that when those in power feel threatened they "push back." Those who have forgotten, or do not wish to comply with, the doctrine of higher authority because they have developed a "god-complex" will often retaliate in either an aggressive or passive-aggressive way. Both biblical and American history bears this out. King Nebuchadnezzar and the King George of England are two historical examples that we will consider in the next chapter.

The central question then becomes this: When are government officials operating under a legal authority, and when have they overstepped their authority and become tyrants?

Before we get ahead of ourselves trying to answer this question, let us first recognize and understand that there is a "Universal Chain-of-Command," often ignored. The root cause of these abuses of power, in fact, is either a lack of understanding, or a complete rejection, of what can be termed, "The Doctrine of Higher Authority" and the "Universal Chain-of-Command."

A Lasting Bulwark
Against Tyranny

What is the Basis for American Liberty?

"And yet the same revolutionary beliefs for which our forebears fought are still at issue around the globe– the belief that the rights of man come not from the generosity of the state but from the hand of God."[49]

~John F. Kennedy

There has been much discussion, even among Christian patriots, about whether to call our American liberties "God-given," "civil" or "constitutional" rights. It seems the lines between these definitions have been blurred, leading to much confusion. Allow me to distinguish these three terms for the sake of what we are trying to accomplish.

God-given Rights–The idea of a right being "God-given" presumes there is a God (Creator) and that all of our rights come directly from Him to every individual. Our Founding Fathers acknowledged this truth in the Declaration of Independence when they stated, "We

---

[49] John F. Kennedy, "Inaugural Address," (Speech: Washington, DC, January 20, 1961), John F. Kennedy Presidential Library and Museum, https://www.jfklibrary.org/Research/Research-Aids/Ready-Reference/JFK-Quotations/Inaugural-Address.aspx

hold these truths to be self-evident, that all men are *created* equal, that they are endowed *by their Creator* with certain *unalienable* Rights."[50]

The political ideology that recognizes God as the *highest authority in every case of law and justice,* and that all of our rights come from this source, will be referred to, for the purpose of this book, as "Americanism." Americanism maintains that our "rights" come from the hands of the Creator. This belief stands in stark contrast to all other forms of political ideology (socialism, communism, Marxism, Nazism, fascism etc.), and has been what has set America apart from every other form of government. It guarantees freedom to the common citizen and outlaws tyranny, placing both a biblical and moral restraint upon corrupt or power-mad civil authorities, who eagerly suppress our inalienable rights.

One can often, in truth, ascertain the ideological persuasion of another person by determining whether or not they advocate and protect these rights. A person may be American by citizenship, for example, but also be a communist or a socialist, at least in regards to their ideology. An atheist, therefore, is not "American" in the genuine ideological sense of the word because he denies the very existence of the Supreme Being, does not acknowledge His authority as Creator and, accordingly, has no basis on which to affirm and protect God-given rights.

The idea that our rights originate from our Creator is what make these rights "inalienable." The word inalienable means that these rights cannot be taken from us or be trampled on, in the ultimate sense, by any earthly or moral power, *even government officials.* Since God has given these rights to all men equally, it is then illogical to assume that any magistrate or bureaucrat has the authority to deprive others of them. As men are created equal, any attempt by civil authorities to control the lives and actions of their fellow man, through laws and arbitrary enforcement, must be clearly *justified by a higher authority, or those very same laws are invalid and illegal.*

---

[50] Thomas Jefferson, *The Declaration of Independence,* Essay, July 4th, 1776, http://teachingamericanhistory.org/library/document/declaration-of-independence/

Constitutional Rights – The phrase "constitutional rights" can be misleading if not understood and defined clearly. As Americans, we have been misled into thinking we have constitutional rights. While we do, *we can appeal to something much higher – we have divine, God-given rights.* And our Founding Fathers had the wisdom and foresight to protect these inalienable rights from the federal government officials by creating a legal document called the U.S. Constitution, which was later amended to include the Bill of Rights.

The U.S. Constitution is the supreme law of the land, and was created in order to curtail and limit the powers of the federal government. Our Founding Fathers had no confidence in government. Thomas Paine epitomized this healthy skepticism in his revolutionary pamphlet *Common Sense*, which states, "Society in every state is a blessing, but Government, even in its best state, is but *a necessary evil; in its worst state an intolerable one.*"[51] The Founders knew all too well what corrupt power does to mankind. Therefore, they created a legal document known as the Constitution, which the American people could later use to restrain the federal government from "usurping" (illegally taking) power that was not granted to it by either man or God.

When we think about why laws are established, we understand they are generally drawn up by government officials to regulate the lives of the citizenry and criminalize certain behavior. The U.S. Constitution and the Bill of Rights, on the other hand, were created *for just the opposite purpose.* These legal documents were created by "We the People", through their representatives, to regulate the actions of federal government officials and criminalize unlawful behavior by the civil authorities. None of the constitutional amendments in the Bill of Rights were intended to restrict the lives of the American people. They restrict the Federal Government. The amendments do not say, "The people shall not...." Rather they say, "Congress shall not...."

The rights that our Founding Fathers sought to protect have always existed, as they were conveyed by the Creator Himself, and are applicable throughout the entire globe, in all countries, and at all times. The Bill of Rights puts a "barrier" around these God-given rights and

---

[51] Thomas Paine, *Common Sense,* Essay, January 9, 1776, Source: Bill of Rights Institute, https://billofrightsinstitute.org/founding-documents/primary-source-documents/common-sense/

serves as a "restraining order" on the federal government. It put a legal fence around our God-given rights, so that the newly created federal government would never be permitted to invade the sovereignty of individual states or impose, with civil penalties, unjust or illegal laws.

In short, American Constitutional law was created to restrain federal officials from suppressing our God-given rights.

Civil Rights – Like the phrase "constitutional rights," the term "civil rights" can also be misleading if its definition is not understood clearly. Webster's 1828 dictionary defines the word *civil* as "relating to the policy and government of the citizens and subjects of a state."[52] A civil right or liberty involves the right of people to do or say things without being stopped, impeded or interrupted by government officials. The difference between a humanistic view of civil rights and a biblical view of God-given rights hinges upon *where these rights originate.*

Under all other ideological systems (socialism, communism, Marxism, fascism, etc.), a citizen may be granted certain rights. These rights arise from the benevolence of the civil authorities and can be taken away and suppressed at any time, at their discretion.

In the American system of government, our rights are God-given, constitutionally protected, and cannot be legally suspended by government officials under *any* circumstances. Our Founding Fathers believed the government's primary responsibility was to secure and protect the rights that God conveyed to His people. If government officials either fail to protect these God-given rights, or worse yet, they themselves strip citizens of these rights, then the people have the right to institute a new government. This is clearly articulated in the Declaration of Independence:

> *That to secure these [God-given] rights, Governments are instituted among Men*, deriving their just powers from the consent of the governed — That whenever any Form of Government becomes destructive of these ends, it is the Right of the People to alter or to

---

[52] *Webster's 1828 English Dictionary,* s.v. "Civil," http://sorabji.com/1828/ words/c/civil.html"

abolish it, and to institute new Government, laying
its foundation on such principles and organizing its
powers in such form, as to them shall seem most
likely to affect their Safety and Happiness.[53]

Just sixty years ago, the Christian church stood silently by as the federal government unconstitutionally kicked prayer and the Bible out of the public schools without understanding the effect this would have on all of our other freedoms. State officials, and their fiat decisions, were now, in essence, replacing God as the highest legal authority. If there is no God or "Creator" who is recognized universally by the American people and their elected representatives as the supreme authority in all matters of law and justice, then politicians and judges will, by default, usurp this power for themselves.

If there is no higher authority than civil government, then the government literally becomes "God" and can determine which rights the people are permitted to enjoy and which rights will be taken away. If our rights do not come from God as stated by the Founding Fathers, then they must necessarily come from the government. This view leads to government-granted privileges called "civil rights" or "human rights," as the atheistic Humanist Manifesto reads. Such rights are flimsy indeed, and can provide no lasting bulwark against tyranny.

---

[53] Thomas Jefferson, *The Declaration of Independence*, Essay, July 4th, 1776, http://teachingamericanhistory.org/library/document/ declaration-of-independence/

The Last Line of Defense

Why a Civil Rights Movement?

*"We have waited for more than 340 years for our **constitutional and God-given rights**."*[54]

~ Martin Luther King, Jr.

For the sake of clarity, we must distinguish between the term "civil rights" and a "civil rights movement." The former term refers to those rights which a person enjoys as a citizen of a state, by the benevolence of his or her leaders. A civil rights movement, on the other hand, results whenever government officials have exceeded their divine and constitutional authority and begin to infringe upon the God-given and constitutionally protected rights of the people. Many times throughout American history, these guaranteed rights have existed on paper, but were not being respected in practice by the civil authorities, who became corrupted by the lust for power. When people are made aware of their rights and come to the realization that their fellow man (the civil authorities) are not respecting them, then opposition in the form of legal action and even social unrest (civil disobedience) will always ensue.

---

[54] Martin Luther King Jr. *Letter From a Birmingham Jail*, April 16, 1963, African Studies Center, https://www.africa.upenn.edu/Articles_Gen/Letter_Birmingham.html

When we study history, we see that Martin Luther King appealed to his God-given and constitutionally protected rights in order to justify his holy cause. This is articulated well in his *Letter from the Birmingham Jail:* "We have waited for more than 340 years for our *constitutional and God-given rights.* The nations of Asia and Africa are moving with jet-like speed toward gaining political independence, but we still creep at horse and buggy pace toward gaining a cup of coffee at a lunch counter."[55]

During the time of Martin Luther King (as it was during the years leading up to the Civil War), it was the state governments that were responsible for violating the God-given rights of their citizens. However, this was the genius of the republican type of government— that if the individual state governments ever infringed upon the God-given rights of their people, they had the option to leave the state in favor of a more "just" government, or they could stay and appeal to the rest of the nation for help.

Alexander Hamilton explained this concept in a speech to the New York Ratifying Convention, June 21 1788: "This balance between the National and State governments," he said, "ought to be dwelt on with peculiar attention, *as it is of the utmost importance.* It forms a double security to the people. If one encroaches on their rights they will find a powerful protection in the other. Indeed, they will both be prevented from overpassing their constitutional limits by a certain rivalship, which will ever subsist between them."[56]

King's cause was victorious because he was operating with both the divine (moral) authority and the existing legal (constitutional) authority. His primary objection was with the "civil government," or to be more precise the "civil authorities," who were guilty of infringing upon these rights of equality. This is why his efforts resulted in what has been called a civil rights movement.

---

[55] Martin Luther King Jr. *Letter From a Birmingham Jail,* April 16, 1963, African Studies Center, https://www.africa.upenn.edu/Articles_Gen/Letter_Birmingham.html

[56] Alexander Hamilton, "First Speech of June 21," (Speech, Poughkeepsie, June 21, 1788) Teaching American History, http://teachingamericanhistory.org/library/document/alexander-hamilton-speech/

These "rights of equality" that King sought to restore can be found in both divine and constitutional law. They can be seen first and foremost in Scripture. This is stated nicely in an article by Dr. John D. Morris, President of the Institute for Creation Research.

It is good to remind ourselves, from time to time, that the foundational charter of America, the Declaration of Independence, is a creationist document. Our founding fathers separated from England by citing the Biblical truth that all men are created equal. This status recognized inalienable human rights granted by the Creator and not by men or governments. The world has benefited by the successful separation, as America has been a source of freedom and hope to many. Most importantly, America has been a nation from which the Gospel has emanated.

But what of the idea that all individual men are created equal? Certainly the circumstances of their birth have not been equal. All have different levels of ability and opportunity. Even access to Gospel truth has not been equal. In what way are we created equal?

Historically, we all come from the same ancestral source. From Noah and his sons 'was the whole earth overspread' (Genesis 9:19). Before that all came from Adam 'the first man' (I Corinthians 15:45-46) and Eve, 'the mother of all living' (Genesis 3:20). There are no others, for God 'hath made of one blood all nations of men' (Acts 17:26). The modern distinction of 'race' is not the Biblical concept in which differences stem from the separation at Babel based solely on 'every one after his tongue, after their families, in their nations' (Genesis 10:5).

Genetically, we are 'equal' as well. Now that the human genome has been deciphered, we know every human is so similar to everyone else that we are all essentially 'clones' of each other. The various expressions we recognize are best understood as designed adaptations.

Personally, we are equal too. The Bible tells us that 'all have sinned, and come short of the glory of God' (Romans 3:23). Thankfully, Christ 'is the propitiation for our sins: and not for our's only, but also for the sins of the whole world' (I John 2:2).

Eternally, we will be evaluated equally; based on our creed, not rank of birth. The unbelieving 'peoples, and multitudes, and nations, and tongues' (Revelation 17:15) are consigned to judgment, while the redeemed believers gather around His throne singing His praises from 'every kindred, and tongue, and people, and nation' (5:9). The unequal rewards or consequences will be due to our choices and conduct after having an equal standing.

Equal rights called for in the Declaration were an extension based on a higher Charter, the Holy Scriptures. If we would fully embrace the Declaration, we must cling to its underlying Document.[57]

The "rights of equality" were also recognized by both federal and constitutional law. Following the American Civil War, Congress passed a law called the Civil Rights Act of 1866, which guaranteed that the newly freed slaves would have rights equal to those of white citizens. This legislation was passed by Congress in 1865, but was vetoed by President Andrew Johnson because he understood that the 10th Amendment to the U.S. Constitution restricted the federal government from passing laws regulating the internal affairs of the

---

[57] John D. Morris, *Are All Men Created Equal?* Article, 2006, Institute for Creation Research, http://www.icr.org/article/are-all-men-created-equal/

sovereign states. The following year, Congress once again passed the bill, which President Johnson again vetoed. However, as required by the U.S. Constitution, the veto was nullified by a two-thirds majority vote in each house of Congress.

To remedy this conflict, Congress passed, and the states ratified (sic), the Fourteenth Amendment to the United States Constitution and its Equal Protection Clause. The clause, which took effect in 1868, forbids states to deny any person within its jurisdiction "the equal protection of the laws."

During the civil rights movement of the 1960s, even though these rights of equality were legally (constitutionally) protected, they only existed *on paper* (both in the Bible, implicitly, and in the Declaration of Independence and the Constitution explicitly). These rights were not being respected *in practice* by the civil authorities in the South. As a result, opposition, legal action and social unrest ensued. The grassroots people, recognizing that their fellow man (the civil authorities) were guilty of illegally, immorally, and unconstitutionally suppressing these God-given and constitutionally protected rights, demanded that the unrighteous oppression come to an end.

These are the steps that must be present in any successful civil rights movements. When confronting government officials, the people must be operating under divine, moral and legal authority. The movement requires the people to rise up and *demand* that the civil authorities quit suppressing or denying their rights through unjust laws, unjust rulings or by using government force to execute unlawful edicts.

This is where we are in America today. Nearly every right given to us by God and legally protected by the Constitution has been usurped (illegally taken) from us. First and foremost, this includes the freedom of religion. The First Amendment to the Constitution legally protects this divine right to pray and *forever forbids* the Federal Government from ever infringing on it: *"Congress shall make no law...prohibiting the free exercise of religion."*[58] Therefore, when the Supreme Court began to ban prayer and the reading of the Bible in the schools, they violated both a God-given and constitution-

---

[58] U.S. Const. Amend I, Sec. 1 Cl. 1

ally protected right. The Supreme Court has and continues to violate both divine and constitutional law. This is an act of tyranny.

The problem is neither with our system of government, nor with the Constitution. The problem is that our fellow citizens (i.e. the civil authorities) have been corrupted with so much political power, that they now consider themselves to be the highest authority on all matters of law and justice. This is being acknowledged by even our own government officials. On November 22, 1994, thirty state governors unanimously adopted the Williamsburg Resolve. In it they said: "The challenges to the liberties of the people... comes from our own Federal government that has defied, and now ignores, virtually every constitutional limit fashioned by the framers to confine its reach and thus to guard the freedoms of the people," and "Federal action has exceeded the clear bounds of... the Constitution, and thus violated the rights guaranteed to the people."[59]

For the last 80 years, most of our elected officials at both the state and federal level have violated their oaths of office and are guilty of either "crimes of commission" or "crimes of omission." Every elected official since the time of the Founding Fathers has sworn to protect the rights of the American people. Every civil official has been required to take the following oath to Almighty God: "I do solemnly *swear* (or affirm) that I will support and defend the Constitution of the United States against all enemies, foreign and domestic; that I will bear true faith and allegiance to the same; that I take this obligation freely, without any mental reservation or purpose of evasion; and that I will well and faithfully discharge the duties of the office on which I am about to enter: *So help me God.*"[60]

The practice of taking this oath began with the first U.S. Congress. Article I, Section 2 of the U.S. Constitution states, "The House of Representatives shall choose their Speaker and *other Officers*."[61] One of the first officers that the Founding Fathers appointed was the Rev.

---

[59] *The Williamsburg* Resolve, November 22, 1994, North Carolina American Republic Resource Library, http://www.ncrepublic.org/lib_williamsburgresolve.php

[60] U.S. Constitution, Art. 2. Sec. I

[61] U.S. Const. Art. 1, Sec. 2, Cl. 5

William Linn as Chaplain of the House on May 1, 1789. The oaths of office were officiated by a clergy member with the understanding that they were not just making a promise to the American people; they were also making a promise to God Himself, a promise that every government official and military veteran would eventually give an account for: "When you make a vow to God, do not delay to pay it; For He has no pleasure in fools. Pay what you have vowed. Better not to vow than to vow and not pay. Do not let your mouth cause your flesh to sin, nor say before the messenger of God that it was an error. Why should God be angry at your excuse and destroy the work of your hands?"[62]

Those elected officials who are guilty of "crimes of commission" are those who actively suppress our rights by illegally expanding the power and reach of the federal government. Those elected officials who are guilty of "crimes of omission" are those who do not support or defend our rights as they have all promised, by oath to God, to do. Many civil servants today have not been guilty of destroying our rights, but are also in no way following through on their promise to protect and defend them, either. Those who are guilty of intentionally and deliberately failing to support and defend the American people from the illegal and unconstitutional encroachment from the federal government will ultimately answer to God for their lies.

When our elected officials, at both the national and local level, refuse to honor their oath to God, and their promise to protect our God-given rights, they are committing an act of perjury which can be punishable by up to five years in prison under federal law.[63] If our government official refuse to protect our rights, then this responsibility falls to the last line of defense: *The individual American citizen.* As former Supreme Court Justice James Byrnes concluded in an article for U.S. News and World Report, "Power intoxicates men. It

---

[62] Eccl 5:4-7 NKJV

[63] *U.S. Code18 U.S.C. § 1621; 28 U.S.C. § 1746*, Office of the United States Attorneys, https://www.justice.gov/usam/criminal-resource-manual-1759-perjury-cases-28-usc-1746-declarations

is never voluntarily surrendered. It must be taken from them."[64] The most effective way to take that power from "them" is to disobey their illegal, immoral and unconstitutional mandates and then petition the Almighty God to arbitrate the dispute.

Defying the unjust and illegal tyranny of corrupted government officials is the only strategy that has historically proven to work. Moses understood and applied this truth. Daniel, Shadrach, Meshach, and Abednego understood and applied this truth. Our Christian Founding Fathers who ended the tyranny of Britain understood and applied this truth. The Christian abolitionists who ended slavery understood and applied this truth. A Christian minister named, Martin Luther King, Jr., who ended government sponsored segregation and discrimination, understood and applied this truth. What truths did they understand and apply to end tyranny? Their actions were three-fold:

1. They all clearly understood and applied the Doctrine of Higher Authority to their cause.
2. They defied and ignored immoral, unjust and illegal laws.
3. They called upon God as an arbitrator, i.e. they Appealed to Heaven.

America is only a matter of years from living under a totalitarian dictatorship because the apathetic American people (and especially the Christian church) has stood idly by as our rights have been systematically and incrementally stripped from us one by one.

Throughout American history, whenever a class of people comes to the realization that their leaders, through a "long train of abuses and usurpations,"[65] have illegally granted themselves absolute power and authority, and have refused to be controlled by men, constitution or laws, they will appeal to their rulers for their rights to be restored. These types of appeals and petitions have historically fallen upon deaf ears, as the rulers refuse to surrender their unauthorized

---

[64] Clifford M. Lytle, *The Warren Court and its Critics*, (Tucson: University of Arizona Press. 1968) 94–95.

[65] Thomas Jefferson, *The Declaration of Independence,* Essay, July 4th, 1776, http://teachingamericanhistory.org/library/document/declaration-of-independence/

and even illegal exercise of power over the people. Therefore, what recourse do a people have when justice is denied by their rulers and there is no higher court or ruler on earth to appeal to? **They may Appeal to the Supreme Court of Heaven**.

Our Founding Fathers essentially cast off an entire system of government (monarchy) and replaced it with an entirely different form of government known as a Constitutional Republic. They accomplished this feat through a revolution, of sorts. A civil rights movement, on the other hand, does not seek to go as far as overthrowing the existing system of government, but rather seeks to restore that which already exists on paper, but is not being respected and adhered to by our civil authorities.

Our "Appeal to Heaven" civil rights movement should not result in secession, revolution or an armed rebellion. In other words, it simply seeks to restore (by legal and constitutional means) the system of government that the Founding Fathers created and that we are guaranteed by God and by Section 4, Clause 1 of the U.S. Constitution—a government that is governed by "the laws of nature and nature's God," and in which the Constitution is the highest legal and moral authority that governs "every soul." This can never be truly understood without a proper and biblical understanding of the relationship between God, government, and the citizens, as articulated in Romans 13 under the **Doctrine of Higher Authority**.

Religious and Political Fear Tactics

Does the Bible Teach a "Divine Right of Kings"?

"Let every soul be subject unto the higher powers. For there is no power (authority) but of God: the powers that be are ordained of God. Whosoever therefore resists the power, resists the ordinance of God: and they that resist shall receive to themselves damnation."[66]

~ Romans 13:1-2

Since we have entered the 21st century, much of the contemporary Christian church in America has become nothing more than an irrelevant social club incapable or unwilling to do what is necessary to return America to righteousness. We have failed to be the "salt" and the "light" of the earth.[67]

The church has lost its place and seems to have abdicated both its political and divine authority. This "divine authority" was given by God the Father to His Son Jesus Christ (Matt 28:18) who in turn gave it to the church (Mark 13:34). Until now, Christians in America had forgotten that they were given the right and the duty to "exhort,

---

[66] Rom 13:1-2 NKJV

[67] Matt 5:13-16 NKJV

and rebuke with all authority"[68] or had been too timid, reluctant or complacent to exercise this right.

In America, all legal authority is derived from one of two sources: **Divine law** and **Constitutional law**. Divine law is the supreme *law of the world*. It is superior in obligation to any other. It is binding over the entire globe, in all countries, and at all times. No human laws are of any validity if contrary to these God-given laws. "Divine" carries the idea there is a *moral authority* higher than even earthly governments and the laws and rulings of government officials. Constitutional law, on the other hand, is the supreme law of the American legal system and carries the idea of *legal authority*. It is second in authority only to divine law.

When running the Appealing to Heaven proposal by some trusted advisors, we were warned to be careful not to violate our responsibility as Christian citizens to submit to civil authorities, established in Romans 13. While this concern was valid, the interpretation of this one passage has become so extreme in some evangelical circles that many now believe Christians must obey all laws, commands and orders given by those in positions of authority (presidents, congressmen and judges), without using any discernment or the "whole council of God"[69] as their guide. Allow me to use my years of experience in law enforcement to illustrate my point.

As a police officer, I was a "civil authority." While operating under the law, I had a tremendous amount of authority granted to me. For example, in a traffic stop I had the authority to pull a person over, order him or her to provide identification, get out of the car, and even submit to a field sobriety test, if I thought the person was under the influence. However, this authority was not without limits. I did not have either the legal or moral authority to order a woman to get out of her car, to get undressed, to submit to unwanted sexual advances, and to use my firearm to force her compliance. This type of abuse of power by civil authorities is what our Founding Fathers called "tyranny." Tyranny could therefore be defined as an arbitrary

---

[68] Titus 2:15 NKJV

[69] Acts 20:27 NKJV

exercise of power by civil authorities over subjects or citizens *that is not authorized by law*.

I do not know of any minister that would tell his wife, "Honey, I know that this government official is acting beyond both his moral and legal authority, but scripture teaches that we are to submit to all civil authorities because they are all appointed by God." We see it is asinine, speaking frankly, to think God expects us blindly to obey all laws, commands and orders given by those in positions of civil authority. The balance then, that we must be careful to maintain, is between those times when we must obey government edicts and when are we permitted and even commanded by God to defy the civil authorities. The key to maintaining this balance comes from the realization that we have the right and even the duty to disobey our civil officials when they themselves are guilty of violating the "Doctrine of Higher Authority" as established in Romans 13.

In order for tyrants to lord it over the people, they must first accomplish one of two agendas (or both). They must:

1. Remove God as the supreme authority, thus making the state supreme. – Or -
2. If they are dealing with a religious people, they must convince them that God requires obedience to the rulers, without qualification or caveat, as an act of obedience to God.

Christian leaders need to guard against the government's misuse of scripture to control and subjugate a Christian population. This was the tactic utilized throughout Christian Europe in the 16th, 17th and 18th centuries, and once again by the Nazi regime, leading to the rise of Hitler. Once Christianity began to spread throughout the world, the "Christian" kings of Europe and their "religious" allies used a flawed interpretation of Roman 13 to develop a teaching called "The Divine Right of Kings." They used it to justify and legitimize their laws and to demand absolute and unquestioned obedience from their subjects.

The so-called "Divine Right of Kings" was a religious and political "fear tactic" used by the tyrants of "Christian Europe." These political leaders would demand blind allegiance and obedience from their subjects, who, if they resisted, would be guilty of violating the will of God and bring damnation upon themselves—or so they were told. In a speech given before Parliament in 1609, King James I made the following remarks with regard to the divine right of kings: "The state of monarchy is the 'supremest' thing upon earth. For kings are not only God's lieutenants upon earth and sit upon earth and sit upon God's throne, but even by God Himself they are called gods."[70]

According to this doctrine, both Romans 13:1-5 and 1 Peter 2:13-15 teach that God has placed the king (or government leaders) in their positions of authority. If a citizen was to defy the laws of a king, they would, accordingly, be committing a sacrilegious act against God Himself. Let us review these scriptures and determine whether or not this interpretation is either biblically or historically valid.

Rom. 13:1-2 reads: "Let every soul be subject unto the higher powers. For there is no power (legal authority) but of God: the powers that be are ordained of God. Whosoever therefore resists the power, resists the ordinance of God: and they that resist shall receive to themselves damnation."[71]

Romans 13:1-2 presupposed several points that need to be explored further if we are to apply these truths to our individual and national lives.

Point #1. "For there is no power (legal authority) but that which has been ordained by God." This is what we call Divine Authority and supersedes *all other authority*. Romans 13 first and foremost acknowledges that in the universal chain-of-command, the LORD Himself is the highest authority. He is our King, our Lawgiver, and our Judge.[72] Acting as the King of kings, the Lord of lords and the Judge of judges, He is the highest authority in every nation and over every government office. Every state executive, every lawmaker and judicial official, finds themselves under this divine authority regardless of whether or not they recognize their place in this universal chain-of-command. Therefore, any and all authority that a

---

[70] King James I of England, "Speech to Parliament" (Speech, England, 1609) http://history.hanover.edu/courses/excerpts/eurjam1.html

[71] Rom 13:1-2 NKJV

[72] Is 33:22 NKJV

government official possesses is a delegated authority. Point #2 must, therefore, be understood in light of point #1.

Point #2. Romans 13 does not say, "Subjects obey your government," as is too often asserted. Rather, it teaches, "Let every soul be subject to the supreme or higher authority." This scripture teaches there is a divine "chain of command" established by God, and every soul is accountable to it. The order of legal authority or "chain of command" is thus:

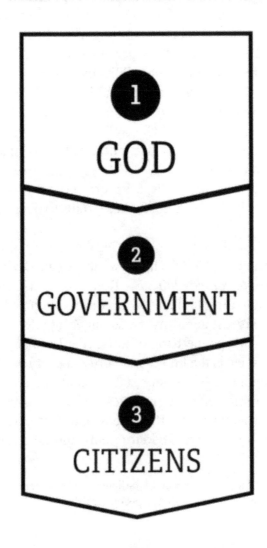

The phrase "every soul" means just that – *every soul*. The challenge throughout history is for every person, whether a common citizen or a king, lord, politician, president, governor or judge to acknowledge their place in the universal chain-of-command and not to overstep their legal authority. Therefore, the divine order, explained in greater detail, is as follows:

1. God as the highest authority. He is all of mankind's King, our Lawgiver, and our Judge regardless of whether or not it is acknowledged by the government official.[73]
2. Government officials are exercising *delegated authority*. When they govern according to biblical principles, laws and commands, they are acting as God's "ministers" and should be given our honor, support and obedience.[74]
3. As Christian citizens, we should submit to the ordinances of man when they do not violate the **Doctrine of Higher Authority**.[75]

This, at times, can be a very complicated subject. When to obey and disobey must be evaluated on a case-by-case basis. William Blackstone, in his Commentaries on the laws of England, makes a clear distinction between those times when man must obey or disobey the civil authorities.

> "To instance in the case of murder; this is expressly forbidden by the divine, and demonstrably by the natural law; and from these prohibitions arises the true unlawfulness of this crime. If any human law should allow or enjoin us to commit it, *we are bound to transgress that human law*, or else we must offend both the natural and the divine. But with regard to matters that are in themselves indifferent, and are not commanded or forbidden by those superior laws;

---

[73] Is 33:22, Romans 13:1-2 NKJV

[74] Romans 13:6-7 NKJV

[75] 1 Peter 2:13-15 NKJV

such, for instance, as exporting of wool into foreign countries; here the inferior legislature has scope and opportunity to interpose."[76]

In the view of Blackstone, if God had already ruled on an issue—like the legality of murder, for example—then the issue was forever settled. However, if God was indifferent and had not ruled on an issue, such as the exporting of wool to China, our elected representatives would then be free to rule on it in a way that would best benefit the nation.

Even as late as the end of the last century, great men at the highest level of the federal government were still echoing these truths. Ronald Reagan said, "Those who created our country—the Founding Fathers and Mothers—understood that there is a *divine order* which transcends the human order."[77]

Under the American system of government, the rights of the individual citizen supersede the laws of the state because these rights come from the hands of the Creator. This historic recognition of the Doctrine of Higher Authority would forever be enshrined in a document known as the Declaration of Independence.

The Declaration was the secessionist document adopted by the Continental Congress on July 4, 1776, which announced to the King of England that the 13 American colonies would no longer be a part of the British Empire. The Declaration of Independence was signed by 56 American leaders between August 2, 1776 and January 22, 1777, including two future presidents, three vice presidents, and ten members of the United States Congress.

The phrase "Declaration of Independence" is never used in the document itself. This document could just as easily have been called "An American Statement of Faith." A statement of faith is a legal document created by a group of likeminded people, enumerating a list of ideas and principles they all believe to be true. In this legal document,

---

[76] Herbert Broom, Edward Alfred Hadley, Sir William Blackstone, "Commentaries on the Laws of England," Volume 1, 1753 Pg. 24

[77] Ronald Reagan, "Remarks at an Ecumenical Prayer Breakfast" (Speech, Dallas, August 23, 1984) Reagan Library, http://www.reagan.utexas.edu/archives/speeches/1984/82384a.htm

the Founding Fathers declare that both our "rights" and our "laws" originate from one divine source–*the Creator*.

Indeed, it is only with this foundational understanding that we can truly understand the difference between a "right" and a "law." **Rights** are things we are permitted by God to do, while **Laws** are things we are forbidden by God to do. Let us now consider the relationship between laws and rights, and their origin, as understood by our Founding Fathers.

Immutable and Inalienable

What is the Connection between Laws and Rights?

"When in the Course of human events, it becomes necessary for one people to dissolve the political bands which have connected them with another, and to assume among the powers of the earth, the separate and equal station to which the Laws of Nature and of Nature's God entitle them... We hold these truths to be self-evident, that all men are created equal, that they are endowed by their Creator with certain unalienable Rights."[78]

~ The Declaration of Independence

The Declaration of Independence openly *declares* that our laws and rights come from a higher authority. In its proper historical context, the document was written to the King of England, explaining the "American" belief (in contrast to the British perspective) that our rights and our laws come from the hands of the Creator, and not from the king or the government. Then, where did our Founding Fathers get this radical political-religious belief? From the Creator Himself.[79]

---

[78] Thomas Jefferson, *The Declaration of Independence,* Essay, July 4th, 1776, http://teachingamericanhistory.org/library/document/declaration-of-independence/

[79] 2 Timothy 3:16 NKJV

Most people assume the Bible places a greater emphasis on laws than on rights. And, in a way, this assumption rings true; laws are explicit in Scripture, whereas rights are implicit. Moreover, there is no specific verse that says, "Here are the rights of man." However, there are still many, many implicit examples of human rights, as derived from the positive law. The Bible is not silent on the issue.

While there are certain rights in scripture that are very explicit (such as women's marital rights in Exodus 21:10-11, or the inheritance rights of the firstborn in Deuteronomy 21:15-17), most rights are implied. For every divine law—every time God imposes a duty or prohibits an action—the governing authorities are bound by them. They cannot command what God has forbidden, or forbid what God has commanded. This is how rights are derived. If God gives men a *duty* to pray, then men also have a *right* to pray. If God *prohibits* murder, then man also has a *right* to not to be murdered—otherwise known as a right to life. Man even retains the divine right to defend himself against the advances of criminals and murderers.

From a theological perspective, the law of God is immutable. From a political perspective, the rights of man are inalienable. The word "inalienable" means these rights cannot be extinguished, 'brushed under the rug' or removed by any mortal power, even civil government officials. The word "immutable" means that God's laws are fixed and permanent, unable to be erased or changed by man. This is why divine laws were not given to Moses on parchment, but rather "written in stone" by the finger of God himself. Let us now examine the founders' understanding of these truths.

Rights

Thomas Jefferson understood that our rights were bestowed by God, and he expressed this idea in the Declaration of Independence: "We hold these truths to be self-evident, that all men are created equal, that they are *endowed by their Creator with certain unalienable Rights*." Since these rights come from God and are deduced from his law, they are, or should be, inviolable. There is no earthly authority that has been authorized by heaven to suppress them. As Alexander Hamilton states in The Farmer Refuted, written in 1775:

> The sacred rights of mankind are not to be rummaged
> for, among old parchments, or musty records. They
> are written, as with a sun beam, in the whole volume
> of human nature, *by the hand of the divinity itself; and
> can never be erased or obscured by mortal power.*[80]

Therefore, since we are all created equal and possess the same rights under the same divine law, our fellow man, even in positions of government, does have the authority to restrict the rights God has conveyed to us. This is what our Founding Fathers called "despotism," which is simply an overstepping of legal authority by government officials. Tyranny, on the other hand, is government enforced despotism—the potent application of despotism on the populace at large. It results whenever government officials abuse power over subjects or citizens in ways not authorized by divine law, and then force illegal mandates upon the people.

Laws

The idea that God (divine law) is the source and basis for all laws was also expressed by Thomas Jefferson in the Declaration of Independence when he used the phrase "Laws of Nature and of Nature's God." Alexander Hamilton, quoting William Blackstone in The Farmer Refuted, explains what these terms mean:

> This is what is called the law of nature, "which,
> being... dictated by God himself, is, of course, supe-
> rior in obligation to any other. It is binding over all
> the globe, in all countries, and at all times. No human
> laws are of any validity, if contrary to this; and such of
> them as are valid, derive all their authority, mediately,
> or immediately, from this original.[81]

---

[80] Alexander Hamilton, "The Farmer Refuted," Essay, February 23, 1775, Teaching American History, http://teachingamericanhistory.org/library/document/the-farmer-refuted/

[81] Alexander Hamilton, "The Farmer Refuted," Essay, February 23, 1775, Teaching American History, http://teachingamericanhistory.org/library/document/the-farmer-refuted/

Let us examine this important, and oftentimes overlooked, phrase in this "American Statement of Faith" in order to understand how the Founders interpreted Romans 13. There are two parts of Jefferson's phrase that we will draw from and consider in detail. Alexander Hamilton's explanation will also help us flesh out the deeper meaning of these important words.

1. "Such of them [laws] that are valid, derive all their authority from this original."–All of history's great leaders have understood and advocated the truth of divinely delegated authority—that according to Romans 13, God is the highest authority and all laws must derive their delegated authority from Him. Indeed, if man passes and enforces laws that are rooted in this divine authority, then violating them is equivalent to breaking God's own ordinances. Man's laws carry authority as long as their source of authority originates from God Himself. That leads to a corollary truth, stated in part two.

2. "No human laws are of any validity, if contrary to this." – If God has forbidden mankind to perform a certain action, then civil government officials have *no authority* to pass laws, or make rulings, that legalize what God has said is illegal.

Our Founding Fathers understood that God's laws are the basis for all human laws and that any laws passed by civil authorities are in fact *invalid* if contrary to the doctrine of higher authority. In April of 1963, Martin Luther King wrote of this divine principle in his "Letter from the Birmingham Jail," providing a biblical grounding to other Christian leaders for his proposed course of action.

> A just law is a man-made code that squares with the moral law or the law of God. An unjust law is a code that is out of harmony with the moral law. To put it in the terms of Saint Thomas Aquinas, an unjust law is a human law that is not rooted in eternal and natural law.[82]

---

[82] Martin Luther King Jr. *Letter From a Birmingham Jail,* April 16, 1963, African Studies Center, https://www.africa.upenn.edu/Articles_Gen/Letter_Birmingham.html

As was stated in the opening chapters, the "Appeal to Heaven" campaign is the phrase, symbol, and prayer that we have established as the new civil rights movement to restore our American Constitutional Republic. We can achieve this goal by restoring a biblical understanding of authority and the proper relationship between the divine order and civil government.

From biblical perspective, this is how one can discern the difference between a legitimate administration of government and an illegitimate administration of government taken from Romans 13. I have used the following four illustrations to show the divine order of the universe and its relationship with civil government.

LAWFUL   UNLAWFUL

1
GOD

2
GOVERNMENT

3
CITIZENS

Illustration #1 shows the proper and lawful chain-of-command when all parties are submitting to the divine order, or the doctrine of higher authority. In our Pledge of Allegiance, we recite the phrase "one nation *under God*," but we have lost sight of the fact that the word "under" means "submitted to in obedience." Psalms 33:12 reads, "Blessed is the nation whose God is the LORD."[83] The Greek word for LORD means "owner" and "master." For a nation to say they are "under God," and yet be unwilling to submit to His divine precepts, is patently unscriptural. Christ asked the question, "But why do you call Me 'Lord, Lord,' and not do the things which I say?"[84] A nation, which truly understands the divine order of the universe, will legislate according to this principle. America was once that type of a nation.

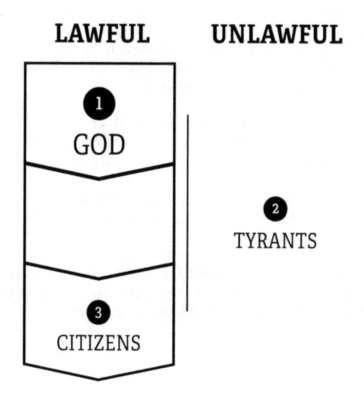

LAWFUL   UNLAWFUL

1

GOD

2

TYRANTS

3

CITIZENS

---

[83] Ps 33:12 NKJV

[84] Luke 6:46 NKJV

71

Illustration #2 shows what happens when government officials begin to pass laws that are not under the divine authority of heaven. This is when civil authorities take themselves out of the divine chain-of-command and become tyrants.

A "tyrant" is a ruler who refuses to be restrained by divine law and has usurped the legitimate sovereignty of heaven. A tyrant is also unworthy of obedience. He has developed a "god-complex" and begins to think he is the sovereign ruler of the universe. He has forgotten that the LORD placed him in his seat of power and that his authority is a delegated authority. In such instances, he may attempt to compel others to follow him in his disobedience, enforcing laws with threats and intimidation. This places the citizens in a no-win or catch-22 situation, and tests them as to whether they will obey the government leaders or be obedient to God.

As William Blackstone notes in his *Commentaries on the Laws of England*, if government officials legalize murder or pass laws forcing us to commit murder, we have both a moral right and a legal obligation to disobey the unjust law, lest we offend God.

> To instance in the case of murder; this is expressly forbidden by the divine, and demonstrably by the natural law; and from these prohibitions arises the true unlawfulness of this crime. If any human law should allow or enjoin us to commit it, we are bound to transgress that human law, or else we must offend both the natural and the divine [law].[85]

The challenge we will consider in the following chapter is what the biblical and moral duty is, and what the responsibility of the citizenry is, when civil government takes this position.

---

[85] Sir William Blackstone, William Gardiner Hammond, *Commentaries on the laws of England*, (Bancroft-Whitney Company, 1890)

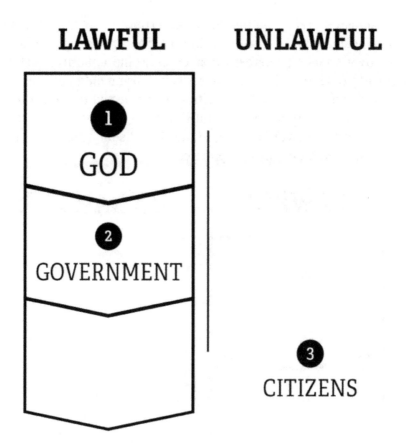

LAWFUL   UNLAWFUL

Illustration #3 show what happens when individual citizens take themselves out from under the divine chain-of-command. Citizens should submit to their rulers only when they are acting under delegated authority. If not, they become lawbreakers. Peter explains: "Therefore submit yourselves to every ordinance of man for the Lord's sake, whether to the king as supreme, or to governors, as to those who are sent by him for the punishment of evildoers and for the praise of those who do good."[86]

Consider again the crime of murder. Since one of the Ten Commandments is "Thou shall not murder," governments have the moral and delegated legal authority to pass laws forbidding murder

---

[86] 1 Peter 2:13-15 NKJV

and imposing civil penalties upon the crime. If a person violates this delegated law, he is, in fact, in rebellion against both God and civil government. "Therefore whoever resists the authority resists the ordinance of God, and those who resist will bring judgment on themselves."[87] Therefore, civil authorities are permitted to punish those who violate the divine order. "But if you do evil, be afraid; for he does not bear the sword in vain; for he is God's minister, an avenger to execute wrath on him who practices evil."[88]

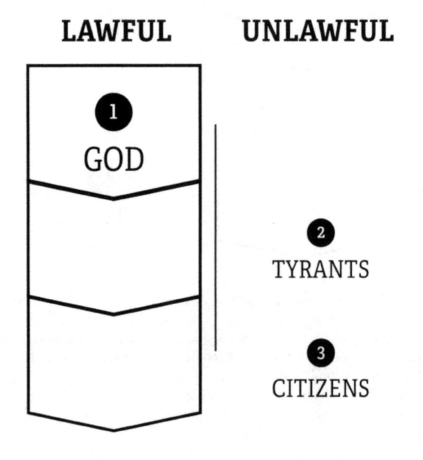

LAWFUL UNLAWFUL

1 GOD

2 TYRANTS

3 CITIZENS

---

[87] Rom 13:2 NKJV

[88] Rom 13:4-5 NKJV

Illustration #4 shows an entire world in rebellion. Unfortunately, America is becoming this type of a nation—a nation that has joined the worldwide rebellion against God and His divine authority. As King David wrote: "Why do the nations rage and the people plot a vain thing? The kings of the earth set themselves, and the rulers take counsel together, against the LORD and against His Anointed, saying, 'Let us break their bonds in pieces and cast away their cords from us.'"[89]

God's law was to limit man's conduct for his own good. Without these divine limitations, anarchy results. Anarchy is defined as "a state of society, when there is no law or supreme power, and individuals do what they please with impunity."[90] The phrase "let us break their bands asunder, and cast away their cords from us" describes the vain attempt of the world's leaders to replace God as the higher authority and create a separation of church and state.

In America today, there have been efforts to remove a display of the Ten Commandments from a courthouse or the Nativity scene from a city square, to eliminate prayer and the Bible from our schools, and to eliminate 'under God' in the Pledge of Allegiance. There has been a wholesale attempt by our federal officials to purge any remembrance of our religious heritage as a nation. The results *will be* disastrous. Contrast the nation that submits to the doctrine of higher authority and the nation that forgets these eternal truths: "Blessed is the nation whose God is the LORD" but "the wicked shall be turned into hell, and all the nations that forget God."[91]

Many Christian leaders believe the American Revolution was a violation of Romans 13. This would be inaccurate. The political ideology of our Founding Fathers stemmed from two sources. As we have seen, their biblical justification and worldview came from an understanding that Romans 13 teaches a universal, eternal chain-of-command, and that the power and authority granted to the people may not be usurped by government officials.

---

[89] Ps 2:1-3 NKJV

[90] *Webster's 1828 English Dictionary,* "Anarchy," http://sorabji.com/1828/words/a/anarchist.html

[91] Ps 33:12, Ps 9:17 NKJV

Therefore, what recourse do a people (American or otherwise) have when their God-given rights are being violated by governing officials? The only recourse is civil disobedience. Yet, hoping to avoid extreme and gross violations ourselves, we must examine the justification and basis for civil disobedience, as well as the mode such disobedience must take. That is the topic of the next chapter.

Historical Examples of Religious Oppression and Tyranny

"Governments have not always been tolerant of religious activity, and hostility toward religion has taken many shapes and forms—economic, political, and sometimes harshly oppressive."[92]

~Chief Justice Warren Burger

A s Justice William Douglas noted, history is full of examples of times when tyrants have used the power of government either to suppress religious freedom, or to force their own beliefs on their subjects, without the divine, legal, or constitutional authority to do so.

The book of Daniel can essentially be used as a legal case study, or a historical and judicial precedent, for what government officials are allowed to do and what they are forbidden from doing. We must, accordingly, consult the book of Daniel to discern whether the government has the authority to "prohibit the free exercise of religion" or to make any law that would restrict the "free exercise thereof."

---

[92] Chief Justice Warren Burger, Walz v. Tax Commission of the City of New York, 397 U.S. 664 (1970), https://www.law.cornell.edu/supremecourt/text/397/664

Religious Oppression and Tyranny in Babylon

A law calls something "right" and therefore, its opposite is wrong. It then imposes civil penalties (fines, jail, even up to death) for any and all violations. King Nebuchadnezzar was the lawmaker in Babylon and was an authoritarian dictator who answered to no man. He was placed on his throne by God Himself and had the sole authority to pass any law he felt necessary to govern his nation. According to the Doctrine of Higher Authority, his was a delegated authority. He had no authority to establish a religion by law other than what was permitted by the supreme Lawgiver. Conversely, in Daniel 3:2-6, he passed a law ordering his subjects to worship his god, the image he had erected, and then imposed civil punishments on those who refused. This was an *establishment of religion*. It was unjust because it violated the "higher law" which reads, "You shall have no other gods before Me. You shall not make for yourself a carved image – any likeness of anything that is in heaven above, or that is in the earth beneath, or that is in the water under the earth; you shall not bow down to them nor serve them."[93]

The three Hebrew children (Shadrach, Meshach and Abednego) understood they had no moral or legal obligation to obey such an unjust law. Their actions demonstrated their belief that there is another King whose laws and commandments are superior to, and supersede, all others, including the established governments of men. As a result, they were labeled as extremists, law-breakers, and non-conformists by the civil authorities and were subjected to civil penalties. Their actions were seen as subversive to the nation since they were not obeying the "laws of the land." They could have responded: "By what authority are you doing these things? And who gave you this authority?" However, this was unnecessary since they already knew the king had no such authority to overrule the commands of heaven. Instead, they simply responded: "O Nebuchadnezzar, we have no need to answer you in this matter."[94] Since the faith of these children required them to obey God over the unjust ruling of man, even under penalty of death, the tyrant was unable to control their actions and God was glorified as a result.

---

[93] Exodus 20:3-5 NKJV

[94] Daniel 3:16 NKJV

Likewise, King Darius was the lawmaker in his kingdom. His governmental power was far less than that of King Nebuchadnezzar, however, since he did not have the authority to change a law once it was enacted. Upon urging from other government officials, he passed a law commanding people not to pray to God for a period of 30 days. His law prohibited the *free exercise of religion*. Even though he was the king, he had no delegated authority from heaven to prohibit prayer. Daniel, who refused to abide by the law, was subsequently labeled an extremist, law-breaker, and non-conformist by the civil authorities and was subjected to civil penalties. Since Daniel's faith required him to obey God over the unjust rulings of man, even under penalty of death, the tyrant was unable to control his actions and once again God was glorified as a result.

In the above passages, the Creator Himself enumerated the jurisdictional limits of all future governments with regard to freedom of religion—that is, what government officials are permitted by heaven to do and what they are forever forbidden to do. Both Nebuchadnezzar and Darius were acting as tyrants because they violated the religious freedoms of their subjects. Our religion, or the duty which we owe to our Creator and the manner of discharging it, can be directed only by reason and conviction, not by force or violence.

The three Hebrew Children would have rather suffered death than subordinate their allegiance to God to the authority of the State. Human governments do not have the authority to suspend or otherwise overrule the commands of God. Therefore, if God was to write a national constitution for Babylon and Persia, it might read as follows:

1. King Nebuchadnezzar shall make no law respecting an establishment of religion
2. King Darius shall make no law prohibiting the free exercise of religion.

By seeking to establish a (false) religion, and by attempting to prohibit the free exercise of religion (prayer), both King Nebuchadnezzar and Darius had become tyrants. For their part, the citizens were not obligated to obey such blatant violations of the Doctrine of Higher Authority. With this divine foundational truth in place, we now come to the founding of the events leading up to the creation of the American civil government.

Understanding the struggle that many believers have been faced with throughout world history, our Founding Father's created the 1st Amendment in order that American Christian never have to suffered death rather than subordinate their allegiance to God to the authority of the State. U.S. Supreme Court Justice William O. Douglas had the following to say about the purpose of the 1st Amendment in the case of *Girouard v. United States:*

> *The victory for freedom of thought recorded in our Bill of Rights recognizes that in the domain of conscience there is a moral power higher than the State. Throughout the ages men have suffered death rather than subordinate their allegiance to God to the authority of the State. Freedom of religion guaranteed by the First Amendment is the product of that struggle.*[95]

Religious Oppression and Tyranny in England

In England, citizens were required by law to attend Anglican Church services, and it was punishable by law to conduct any service, or even to address a congregation or hold a religious meeting, without government approval. In early 1664, the English Parliament passed the Conventicles Act that actually made it illegal to hold "bible studies" of more than five people.[96] Those who disagreed with this "establishment of religion by law," or with the government preventing the "free exercise" of their faith, were labeled as extremists, law-breakers, and non-conformists by the civil authorities (the king) and were subjected to civil penalties.

The non-conformist John Bunyan, who understood the rightful scope of authority granted to human government, was imprisoned for

---

[95] Supreme Court Justice William O. Douglas, *Girouard v. United States,* April 22, 1946.

[96] Steve Weaver, "Baptists and 1662: The Persecution of John Norcott and Hercules Collins," Founders, 2012, http://founders.org/fj89/baptists-and-1662-the-persecution-of-john-norcott-and-hercules-collins/

violating the British law. Bunyan stated, "I will stay in jail to the end of my days before I make a butchery of my conscience."[97] God was clearly not sanctioning the laws that suppressed religious freedom. Therefore, if God was to write a national constitution for the governing officials in Britain, it might read as follows:

1. **King Charles II shall make no law respecting an establishment of religion**
2. **King Charles II shall make no law prohibiting the free exercise of religion.**

Understanding that Human governments have neither the authority nor the right to overrule the commands of God, the American colonists fled from religious persecution. They did so with the conviction that religion, or the duty we owe our Creator and the manner of discharging it, can be directed only by reason and conviction, not by force and violence.

A short tour of American history will prove that the leading sentiment among the American colonists was to grant freedom of religion to individual believers and to create a system in which governing officials would be prevented or forbidden, *by Constitutional law*, from ever persecuting citizens for their faith and obedience to Jesus Christ.

America before the Revolutionary War

The Reformation was preceded by the discovery of America: As if the Almighty graciously meant to open a sanctuary to the persecuted in future years, when home should afford neither friendship nor safety.[98]

— Thomas Paine, *Common Sense*

---

[97] Martin Luther King Jr. *Letter From a Birmingham Jail*, April 16, 1963, African Studies Center, https://www.africa.upenn.edu/Articles_Gen/Letter_Birmingham.html

[98] Thomas Paine, *Common Sense*, Essay, January 9, 1776, Source: Bill of Rights Institute, https://billofrightsinstitute.org/founding-documents/primary-source-documents/common-sense/

With these historical and legal precedents in mind, we must remember that America was birthed by Christian refugees who understood the Doctrine of Higher Authority and used it to govern every aspect of their lives, including the affairs of civil government. This can be seen as early as 1620 in the *Mayflower Compact*, in which the Separatists, after leaving England, established a base for the advancement of the Christian faith: "In the name of God, Amen.... Having undertaken, for the Glory of God, and advancements of the Christian faith and honor of our King and Country, a voyage to plant the first colony in the Northern parts of Virginia, do by these presents, solemnly and mutually, in the presence of God, and one another, covenant and combine ourselves together into a civil body politic."[99]

By 1636, government officials in the state of Maryland were required to take the following oath: "I will not, by myself or any other, and directly or indirectly, trouble or molest any person professing to believe in Jesus Christ for or in respect of religion.... I will protect the person molested and punish the offender."[100] From the beginning, the American colonists were committed not only to religious freedoms, but also to protecting basic human rights.

One truth about our Founding Fathers that the secular establishment would have us forget is the qualifications for holding public office in the 17th century. According to *The Story of Our Nation*, the Connecticut settlements of "Hartford, Windsor, Wethersfield, Springfield and Saybrook" each required, in 1639, that there "be complete religious freedom except that the governor must be a church member."[101] The faith of these same settlers can be seen in The Fundamental Orders of Connecticut, a document often credited as being the first written constitution of the New World:

---

[99] *Mayflower Compact,* Agreement, November 11, 1620, Teaching American History, http://teachingamericanhistory.org/library/document/mayflower-compact/

[100] Michael Farris, *The History of Religious Liberty: From Tyndale to Madison*, (Arkansas: Master Books, 2007)

[101] Mary Celeste, *The Story of our Nation*, (New York: The Macmillan Company, 1940) 76

For as much as it hath pleased Almighty God by the wise disposition of his divine providence so to order and dispose of things that we the Inhabitants and Residents of Windsor, Hartford and Wethersfield are now cohabiting and dwelling in and upon the River of Connecticut… were a people are gathered together the word of God requires that to maintain the peace and union of such a people there should be an orderly and decent Government established according to God… to maintain and preserve the liberty and purity of the Gospel of our Lord Jesus which we now profess, as also, the discipline of the Churches, which according to the truth of the said Gospel is now practiced amongst us; *as also in our civil affairs* to be guided and governed according to such Laws, Rules, Orders and Decrees.[102]

A little over 20 years later, the settlers wrote the Connecticut Colony Charter of 1662, which was written to "Invite the Natives of the Country to the knowledge and obedience of the only true God and Savior of mankind, and the Christian faith."[103]

Founding Fathers

I have sworn upon the Altar of God eternal hostility against every form of tyranny over the mind of man.[104]

— Thomas Jefferson

---

[102]*Fundamental Orders of Connecticut,* January 14, 1639, Lonang Institute, http://lonang.com/library/organic/1639-foc/

[103]*Charter of Connecticut,* 1662, Yale Law School, http://avalon.law.yale.edu/17th_century/ct03.asp

[104]Thomas Jefferson, *Letter to Dr. Benjamin Rush,* Monticello, September 23, 1800, National Archives, http://founders.archives.gov/documents/Jefferson/01-32-02-0102

By the year 1640, America began to see a great influx of Christians from all over Europe. America was seen by many Christians as a refuge where they would be able to practice their faith, free from government intrusion. Thomas Paine wrote of this in *Common Sense*: "The Reformation was preceded by the discovery of America: As if the Almighty graciously meant to open a sanctuary to the persecuted in future years, when home should afford neither friendship nor safety."[105]

This migration of believers did not consist merely of one denomination. The believers that came to America were Baptists, Quakers, Mennonites, Presbyterians, Lutherans, Catholics and Methodists. The Irish Presbyterians settled in Pennsylvania, while the French Protestants settled in the Carolinas with the French Huguenots, the Scottish Presbyterians, and the Swedish Protestants.

Recognizing that America was being flooded with refugees from all over Europe, Thomas Paine wrote the following to American Christians in *Common Sense*: "We claim brotherhood with every European Christian, and triumph in the generosity of the sentiment.... It affords a larger field for our Christian kindness; were we all of one way of thinking, our religious dispositions would want matter for probation; and on this liberal principle I look on the various denominations among us to be like children of the same family, differing only in what is called their Christian names."[106]

One of the many facts excluded from American history is that American democracy today is due to the preaching of Christian's ministers in the 1600s. As explained by a public school history textbook called *The Nation's History*, written in 1928: "Thomas Hooker, pastor of the church at Newton, preached a great political sermon in which he argued that governments owe their authority to the consent

---

[105]Thomas Paine, *Common Sense*, Essay, January 9, 1776, Source: Bill of Rights Institute, https://billofrightsinstitute.org/founding-documents/primary-source-documents/common-sense/

[106]Thomas Paine, *Common Sense*, Essay, January 9, 1776, Source: Bill of Rights Institute, https://billofrightsinstitute.org/founding-documents/primary-source-documents/common-sense/

of the people. This was a new idea in the 17th century, and Hooker has been called the 'Father of American Democracy.'"[107]

A study of the many state constitutions that existed before the Federal Constitution should give a sense of American sentiments at the time the Declaration of Independence. In fact, many of the same men helped draft both documents. Their many references to "Christian" and "Protestant" should sufficiently debunk the lie that they were either irreligious or deists.[108]

Although Virginia and Rhode Island guaranteed religious freedom in their state constitutions, and the Northwest Ordinance of 1787 included a Bill of Rights guaranteeing religious freedom in the territories, the Constitutional Convention did not adopt a statement concerning religious freedom. The only time the subject of religion specifically arises in the text of US Constitution is in Article VI. In setting qualifications for federal office, the delegates determined that "No religious Test shall ever be required as a Qualification to any Office or public trust under the United States."[109] This omission of a Bill of Rights nearly prevented ratification of the Constitution. As a remedy, James Madison, borrowing heavily from the Virginia Declaration of Rights, authored in large part by Thomas Jefferson, drafted a Bill of Rights for consideration by the first Congress

The First Amendment was not originally worded as it reads today. Indeed, its wording was one of the hottest debates at the Constitutional Convention, and it previously took many other forms, which together indicate what the Founders were hoping to achieve. Their primary concern, as it turns out, was that the new federal government might arbitrarily create a national religion with the force of law behind it. Accordingly, some early draft amendments spelled this concern out in greater detail. Stated differently, the US Constitution was enacted

---

[107] Arthur Leonard and Bertha Jacobs, *The Nation's History,* (New York: Henry Holt and Company, 1924) 97

[108] *1776 Constitution of Virginia (XVI); the 1776 Constitution of Maryland (XXXIII); the 1776 Constitution of North Carolina (XXXII); the 1776 Constitution of Pennsylvania (II); the 1777 Constitution of Georgia (ART. VI); and the 1778 Constitution of South Carolina (XII).*

[109] U.S. Const. Art. VI, Sec. 1, Cl. 3

so the federal government would never have the authority to force a person to violate their rights of religious conscience.

The Founding Father's Endorsed the Christian Religion

America's Founding Fathers never forbade official endorsements of religion, but simply the establishing of a religion by law. In fact, most of them openly endorsed the Christian religion. Consider the following examples.

George Washington not only endorsed Christianity to the American Indians, but he also stated that the U.S. Congress would work toward this goal: "You do well to wish to learn our arts and ways of life, and above all, the religion of Jesus Christ. These will make you a greater and happier people than you are. Congress will do everything they can to assist you in this wise intention; and to tie the knot of friendship and union so fast, that nothing shall ever be able to lose it."[110]

Similarly, on April 12, 1778, Washington endorsed religious observance by giving a General Orders that the following Wednesday be reserved as a day of prayer and fasting, and that the military chaplains prepare suitable messages for the troops. When Congress authorized this day of fasting, Washington gave a general order to his soldiers, which read, "The Honorable Congress having thought proper to recommend to The United States of America to set apart Wednesday the 22nd. instant to be observed as a day of Fasting, Humiliation and Prayer, that at one time and with one voice the righteous dispensations of Providence may be acknowledged and His Goodness and Mercy toward us and our Arms supplicated and implored; The General directs that this day also shall be religiously observed in the Army, that no work be done thereon and that the Chaplains prepare discourses suitable to the Occasion."[111]

---

[110]George Washington, *The Writings of Washington,* Edited by John C. Fitzpatrick, (Washington: Government Printing Office, 1932), Vol. XV, 55

[111]*General Orders*, Letter, April 12, 1778, National Archives, http://founders. archives.gov/documents/Washington/03-14-02-0450

Washington also believed in the importance of religion for the continued success of republican government. His 1796 Farewell Address, written by Alexander Hamilton[112] and revised by himself, claimed that a whole nation could not long stay moral without religion, that national morality is necessary for good government, and that politicians should cherish religion for the support it gives to the same:

> Of all the dispositions and habits, which lead to political prosperity, Religion and Morality are indispensable supports. In vain would that man claim the tribute of Patriotism, who should labor to subvert these great pillars of human happiness, these firmest props of the duties of Men and Citizens. The mere Politician, equally with the pious man, ought to respect and to cherish them. A volume could not trace all their connections with private and public felicity. Let it simply be asked, Where is the security for property, for reputation, for life, if the sense of religious obligation desert the oaths, which are the instruments of investigation in Courts of Justice? And let us with caution indulge the supposition, that morality can be maintained without religion. Whatever may be conceded to the influence of refined education on minds of peculiar structure, reason and experience both forbid us to expect, that national morality can prevail in exclusion of religious principle. It is substantially true, that virtue or morality is a necessary spring of popular government. The rule, indeed, extends with more or less force to every species of free government. Who, that is a sincere friend to it, can look with indifference upon attempts to shake the foundation of the fabric?[113]

---

[112]"George Washington's Farewell Address," Library of Congress, June 28th, 2016, https://www.loc.gov/rr/program/bib/ourdocs/farewell.html

[113]George Washington, *Farewell Address,"* Essay, September 19, 1796, Teaching American History, http://teachingamericanhistory.org/library/document/farewell-address

The Treaty of Paris ended the war between Great Britain and the American colonies, and the Continental Congress issued a proclamation concerning the cessation of arms. By April 15th, the preliminary articles of peace were approved by Congress. By January 14, 1784, the Treaty of Paris was formally ratified. What is known as "The Definitive Treaty of Peace", is a poignant example of a formal government endorsement of the Christian religion. The peace treaty begins: "In the name of the most holy and undivided Trinity..."[114]

On July 13, 1787, The Continental Congress passed the Northwest Ordinance, which both endorsed religion and protected religious liberty. Relevant portions of the text read:

> And, for extending the fundamental principles of civil and religious liberty, which form the basis whereon these republics, their laws and constitutions are erected; to fix and establish those principles as the basis of all laws, constitutions, and governments, which forever hereafter shall be formed in the said territory. **Art. 1.** No person, demeaning himself in a peaceable and orderly manner, shall ever be molested on account of his mode of worship or religious sentiments, in the said territory... **Art. 3.** Religion, morality, and knowledge, being necessary to good government and the happiness of mankind, schools and the means of education shall forever be encouraged.[115]

19th Century View of Religion

As we have learned, the First Amendment forbade the federal government from ever infringing on the religion liberties of the people. The establishment clause *was not* an attempt by our Founding Fathers to secularize the government. Even by the mid-1800s, the

---

[114]*Treaty of Paris,* Treaty, January 14, 1884, Library of Congress, https://memory.loc.gov/cgi-bin/ampage?collId=lljc&fileName=026/lljc026.db&recNum=28

[115]*Northwest Ordinance*, July 13, 1787, Teaching American History, http://teachingamericanhistory.org/library/document/northwest-ordinance/

U.S. Congress still endorsed the Christian faith and encouraged its growth. If the Founders thought for a minute that the Revolutionary War would have resulted in an attack on Christianity, they would never have allowed it to take place. And they would have met any such suggestion with universal indignation.

The following report from a House of Representatives judiciary committee on March 27, 1854, demonstrates what the Founders would have thought of an attack on the Christian faith:

> At the time of the adoption of the Constitution and the amendments, the universal sentiment was that Christianity should be encouraged, not any one sect [denomination]. Any attempt to level and discard all religion would have been viewed with universal indignation. The object was not to substitute Judaism or Mohammedanism [Islam], or infidelity [atheism], but to prevent rivalry among [Christian] sects to the exclusion of others.... in this age there can be no substitutes for Christianity: that, in its general principles, is the greatest conservative element on which we must rely for the purity and permanence of free institutions. That was the religion of the founders of the republic, and they expected it to remain the religion of their decedents.[116]

The report continues:

> Madison was a member of the convention framing the Constitution, of the convention proposing the amendment, and of Congress when adopted; and yet neither Madison nor Monroe ever uttered a word or gave a vote to indicate that the appointment of chaplains was unconstitutional.... Down to the Revolution, every colony did sustain religion in some form. It was deemed peculiarly proper that the religion of liberty

---

[116]Mr. Meacham, report to the Congress of the United States, page 169, in: America's God and Country: Encyclopedia of Quotations, William Federer, 1994.

should be upheld by a free people. [Christianity] then must be considered as the foundation on which the whole structure rests. Laws will not have permanence or power without the sanction of religious sentiment,– without a firm belief that there is a Power above us that will reward our virtues and punish our vices. In this age there can be no substitute for Christianity: that, in its general principles, is the great conservative element on which we must rely for the purity and permanence of free institutions. That was the religion of the founders of the republic, and they expected it to remain the religion of their descendants. There is a great and very prevalent error on this subject in the opinion that those who organized this Government did not legislate on religion.[117]

A month later (May 1854) in the Thirty-Fourth Congress assembled, Nathaniel P. Banks of Massachusetts, being Speaker of the House, oversaw the passage of a resolution in the House of Representatives, which declared:

Whereas, The people of these United States, from their earliest history to the present time, have been led by the hand of a kind Providence, and are indebted for the countless blessings of the past and present, and dependent for continued prosperity in the future upon Almighty God; and whereas the great vital and conservative element in our system is the belief of our people in the pure doctrines and divine truths of the gospel of Jesus Christ, it eminently becomes the representatives of a people so highly favored to acknowledge in the most public manner their reverence for God.[118]

---

[117]Mr. Meacham, report to the Congress of the United States, page 169, in: America's God and Country: Encyclopedia of Quotations, William Federer, 1994.

[118]Nathaniel P. Banks, *Journal of the House of Representatives of the United States*, Vol. 35, Issue I, 55

Contemporary Examples
of Religious Oppression
and Tyranny

*"By what authority are you doing these things? ...
And who gave you this authority?"*[119]

— Matthew 21:23

A s explained in previous chapters, the political ideology of "Americanism" grounds our rights and laws in the Creator Himself, and it insists that all levels of government take notice. From the landing of the Pilgrims in 1620 until the early 1960s, this ideology defined the governance of our nation and could be summed up in one simple prayer: "Your kingdom come, Your will be done on, earth as it is in heaven."[120] Indeed, the right of the American people to live as "one nation under God" was also a formal commitment to live according to the divine order of the universe. The U.S. Constitution, additionally, was created to protect these rights in case the newly created government should ever attempt to suppress them. The American colonists understood that simply ridding themselves of the King of England and replacing him with an elected legislature

---

[119]Matt 21:23 NKJV

[120]Luke 11:2 NKJV

was not enough to *guarantee* that their own fellow citizens, now drunk with power, would not eventually become tyrants themselves.

In the film *The Patriot*, the character played by Mel Gibson was asked to join the revolutionary army and help end tyranny. In response, he asked a very simple but important question: "Why should I trade one tyrant 3,000 miles away for 3,000 tyrants one mile away? An elected legislature can suppress a man's rights as easily as a King can." This question typifies a fear, so common at the time, that the federal government would itself ignore the rights of the people. A list of guarantees known as the Bill of Rights was created, therefore, with one express purpose in mind: to protect these same rights from the arbitrary power of the elites. The most precious of these rights was the freedom of religion.

However, it still remained possible for the powerful and strong to use brute force against the weak, even without having the requisite authority. After all, a bully may use his power (physical strength) to extort the milk money from your six-year-old child even if he has no right to do so. Without this legal authority, the bully then becomes a criminal. When government officials use physical strength, intimidation, and threats (the police, the army or the courts) to enforce civil penalties (fines, jail or death) without the rightful authority to do so, it is an abuse of power known as tyranny.

When the American people become universally ignorant of the Doctrine of Higher Authority, it becomes much too easy for sophists and demagogues to claim they have the authority to control every aspect of your lives. Consider this simple illustration.

If a person was to walk into your house and notice you were eating nothing but junk food, he or she, in an attempt to protect you from your unwise choices, might say, "I forbid you from eating junk food." How would you respond to this? Your best response would be with a question that was posed to Jesus: "By what authority are you doing these things? And who gave you this authority?"[121] In other words, as my fellow citizen, who gave you the authority to tell me what I can and cannot eat?

---

[121]Matt 21:23 NKJV

The above question would force them to establish the most basic of facts—their authority to forbid your actions in the first place. This would make them defend their authority to control your dietary choices. In an evasive manner, however, they may employ an old lawyer's trick and make you defend your food choice. They might respond by saying: "Do you think that eating all this junk food is good for you? A bevy of medical studies have proven that eating this type of diet will significantly shorten your life." This would put you on the defensive by making you defend your food choice. But this is not the prime issue, nor should it be. The central issue is their authority to tell you what you can and cannot eat. The trick is not to defend your food choice, but rather to take them back to the original question, thus putting them on the defensive: "By what authority are you doing these things? And who gave you this authority?"

Before you concede your rights to another person, you must first require them to justify their authority over some aspect of your life. Once it is established that they have no authority to restrict your food choices, then they can try to persuade you to voluntarily surrender your right to eat junk food for your own good. This simple illustration also applies to all of our civil authorities, up to and including the Supreme Court of the United States (SCOTUS). Therefore, whenever any government official tries to restrict any aspect of your life, your first response should be: "By what authority are you doing these things? And who gave you this authority?" If they are unable to prove that they have the authority to restrict your actions, then you are under no obligation to obey them, thus retaining your rights.

The most fundamental of American rights is our freedom of religion. It was the first right our Founding Fathers sought to protect. Since freedom of religion is a right bestowed upon us by the Creator himself, it is therefore illegal for your fellow man (including any government official) to infringe on it. Therefore, when a government official, including the Supreme Court, seeks to suppress your religious freedoms, your response should be, "By what authority are you doing these things? And who gave you this authority?"

Constitutionally Preventing Religious Oppression and Tyranny

"Congress shall make no law respecting an establishment of religion or prohibiting the free exercise thereof."[122]

~ First Amendment to the Constitution

The U.S. Constitution is the law of the nation. Every government official is subject to its mandates, which means none of them have the authority to transgress its limits. When we think about why laws are typically established, we understand that they are generally intended to regulate the lives of citizens and criminalize certain behavior. The US Constitution and the Bill of Rights, on the other hand, were *created for just the opposite purpose*. They were created by "We the People" to regulate government officials, should they ever attempt to suppress the rights of the people.

None of the constitutional amendments in the original Bill of Rights were intended to restrict the lives of the American people. Rather, they were meant to *restrict the power of the Federal Government*. The amendments do not say, "The people shall not..." Instead, they say *"Congress shall not..."* The Constitution, and especially the Bill of Rights, was not created as an instrument for

---

[122]U.S. Const. Amd. I, Sec. I, Cl. I

government to restrain the people; it is a legal document for the people to restrain the government—lest it come to dominate our lives and our interests. Unfortunately, the SCOTUS has used this same Constitution against the people. Now the document is used as a legal hammer (instrument) not for the people to restrain the government, but rather for government to restrain the rights and freedoms of the people.

As we have learned, freedom of religion is not just an "American" truth, but an eternal one. Our Founding Fathers recognized that all governmental authority was a *delegated authority*. Therefore, even the creation of the religious clauses of the First Amendment had to derive its authority from scripture and had to be justified by biblical precedents. Thus, the "establishment clause" and the "free exercise clause" were created by the first congress to prevent future federal lawmakers and judges from ever establishing "religion by law" or "preventing the free exercise" of religion. The First Amendment reads, "Congress shall make no law respecting an establishment of religion, or prohibiting the free exercise thereof..." Where would the Founders get such a radical and revolutionary idea? They got it from the Creator himself. Therefore, it is paramount that we understand what precipitated the final drafting of this same amendment.

The Bill of Rights was to serve as a *restraining order*, of sorts, should our elected officials ever seek to deprive us of our rights. The first right to be safeguarded was freedom of religion. James Madison, who is often called "The Father of the Constitution", explains this further:

> That Religion or duty we owe to our Creator, and the manner of discharging it, being under the direction of reason and conviction only, not of violence or compulsion, all men are equally entitled to the full and free exercise of it accord[in]g to the dictates of Conscience; and therefore that no man or class of men ought, on account of religion to be invested

with peculiar emoluments or privileges; nor subjected
to any penalties or disabilities unless under.[123]

According to Thomas Jefferson, in his letter to the Danbury
Baptists, the original intent of his "separation of church and state"
was to keep the federal government out of the religious lives of the
states, *not to secularize the nation by federal mandate.*[124]

There are two side-by-side "religious clauses" of the 1st
Amendment of the Constitution. First, Congress shall make no law
respecting an establishment of religion, and second Congress shall
make no law prohibiting the free exercise of religion. Clearly, these
restrictions do not apply to the American people, but rather to the
federal government alone.

Endorsement v. Establishment: A Legal Word Game

*"Congress shall make no law respecting an establish-
ment of religion..."*[125]

— First Amendment to the Constitution

The American people, and especially the Christian church, have
been duped into surrendering religious freedoms by way of legal
word games. Unfortunately, the judicial system has been hijacked
by corrupt lawyers and judges, who bear primary responsibility for
retarding the constitutional protections of our most precious human
rights—especially the right to worship our creator as the supreme
Judge of the world.

A subversive anti-American legal organization known as the
American Civil Liberties Union (ACLU) bears much responsibility

---

[123]James Madison, "The Papers of James Madison:, ed. William T.
Hutchinson and William M. E. Rachal (Chicago: University of
Chicago Press, 1962), 174

[124]Thomas Jefferson, *Letter to the Danbury Baptists*, January 1, 1802, Library of
Congress, https://www.loc.gov/loc/lcib/9806/danpre.html

[125]U.S. Const. Amd. I, Sec. I, Cl. I

for the eradication of religious freedoms in America. Their tactic has been to substitute one word with another, thus changing the entire meaning of the relevant clause. Unfortunately, many other lawyers, many of them Christian, have fallen for this subtle trick. Likewise, the SCOTUS has essentially rewritten the First Amendment without permission from the American people and, has changed our entire system of government. A clause meant to protect religious freedoms is now used to restrict those very freedoms. The SCOTUS rulings have perverted the constitutional text from "government shall not establish a religion by law" to now read "government shall not endorse religion." There is a very big difference between *establishing a religion* and *endorsing religion*.

To establish a religion by law is to regulate the religious lives of citizens and enforce these laws with civil penalties (fines, jail, or death). Both King Nebuchadnezzar and King George were guilty of establishing religions by law and enforcing these same laws with civil penalties. This is explicitly forbidden by the U.S. Constitution. On the other hand, a simple **endorsement of religion** carries no force of law and therefore carries no civil penalties. The word "endorse" is defined as "to declare one's approval or public support of." The ACLU's website shows how these two meanings have been swapped: "The fundamental principle underlying all these decisions is that the Constitution commands that public schools may not take sides in matters of religion and may not endorse a particular religious perspective or any religion at all."[126] Despite the fact that the U.S. Constitution never outlaws the endorsement of religion, but only the establishment of a religion by law. Consider the difference by way of the following illustration.

Tim Tebow endorses Jockey underwear. His endorsement is a declaration of his approval of this product. He has not established, "by law", the wearing of Jockey underwear, much less enforced this law with civil penalties. Endorsement would be: "Hey! These are great undergarments. I recommend them!" Establishment by law would be, "Everyone will be required to wear Jockey underwear.

---

[126]"The Establishment Clause And Public Schools," ACLU, 2016, https://www.aclu.org/establishment-clause-and-schools-legal-bulletin

Anyone not wearing the prescribed underwear or found wearing any other brand will be subject to $50,000 in fines and up to 6 months in jail." This may seem an overly extreme (or amusing) example, but it captures well the conceptual difference. As we proved in the last chapter, the Founding Fathers "endorsed" Christian religion in many government documents such as the Declaration of Independence, The Treaty of Paris, and the Northwest Ordinance.

Religious Oppression and Tyranny in Modern America

The assault on our rights began over half a century ago when the Supreme Court removed God and prayer out of our public schools, even though the First Amendment forbids the government from ever "prohibiting the freedom of religion or abridging the freedom of speech, or the freedom of press."

If an atheistic society was the original intent of our Founding Fathers, then why did the government endorse the Christian faith for over 100 years? Why were there no constitutional issues associated with this practice? How did the American people get by in permitting school prayer, teaching the Bible in classes and saying prayer at football games? How did this happen?

In the early 1960s, America experienced a silent and (virtually) bloodless coup d'état. A coup d'état is defined as a sudden and illegal seizure of the government by a small group of the existing establishment in order to depose another strata of officials and replace them with a new ruling body. The U.S. Supreme Court, acting tyrannically, essentially fulfilled the warning contained in Psalms 2:1-3: "Why do the nations rage, and the people plot a vain thing? The kings of the earth set themselves, and the rulers take counsel together, Against the LORD and against His Anointed, saying, 'Let us break their bonds in pieces and cast away their cords from us.'"[127]

The decision of the Supreme Court to remove prayer and Bibles from public schools was a rejection of the Doctrine of Higher Authority and an act of tyranny. As King Nebuchadnezzar did before them, they forgot their place in the divine chain-of-command. The church's failure

---

[127]Psalms 2:1-3 NKJV

to respond, unlike men and women of faith in the past, allowed this illegal and unconstitutional seizure of power to take place.

Yet, while we like to point to the court cases of 1961 and 1962, the wheels came off the year prior. For roughly 300 years, those serving in the public sector in Maryland were required by their state constitution to take an oath acknowledging their faith in God. This constitutional requirement continued from 1636 until 1961, when the Supreme Court decided this tradition, previously unchallenged, was in violation of the U.S. Constitution, even though the Maryland constitution predates the Constitutional Convention. Apparently, the Founders, to say nothing of the Maryland delegates, did not see a conflict between the two documents.

The requirement that all civil servants swear to their faith in God was not merely an affirmation of His existence, but also of the Doctrine of Higher Authority. It was a public acknowledgement, given under oath, when they understood they were operating under *delegated authority*. Clearly, the American people once had a much deeper view of faith than the very shallow definition held by present-day America.

The liberal Court decided the Maryland tradition, which had gone unchallenged for over 300 years, was in violation of the First Amendment. As we have covered extensively, this was not the intention of our Founding Fathers. The religious clauses of the First Amendment of the Constitution have two parts. In two Supreme Court rulings, the majority opinion twisted the meaning of the first clause (the establishment clause) to invalidate the second (the free exercise clause).[128]

In the conclusion of Justice Potter Stewart, who wrote the dissenting opinions in both the Pennsylvania and New York cases, there are areas in which a doctrinaire reading of the Establishment Clause," he noted, "leads to irreconcilable conflict with the Free Exercise Clause."

---

[128]*School District of Abington Township v. Schempp, 374 U.S. 203*, 1963, Justia, https://supreme.justia.com/cases/federal/us/374/203/case.html and *Engel v. Vitale, 370 U.S. 421*, 1962, Justia, https://supreme.justia.com/cases/federal/us/370/421/case.html

When Justice Stewart subsequently accused the Court of a "doctrinaire reading of the establishment clause," he was repeating a charge once leveled by Jesus against the Pharisees, who had "made the commandment of God of no effect" through their tradition.[129] Whenever the Supreme Court forbids the citizenry from praying, reading the bible in school, or displaying the Ten Commandments, they ignore the import of the free exercise clause. Just as the doctrinaire interpretations of the Sanhedrin nullified the Mosaic Law, so also the doctrinaire interpretation of the establishment clause, as propagated by the Supreme Court, has essentially nullified the Free Exercise Clause. In other words, by your traditions, or prior rulings and legal precedents, you have made the free exercise clause of no effect.

These Supreme Court rulings allowed our government to be infiltrated by Communist principles. The myth of the "separation of Church and State" is oftentimes quoted in support of this change, but this same phrase never appears in the U.S. Constitution. Would you like to know in which constitution the phrase does appear? The Constitution of the United Soviet Socialist Republics of 1936 reads as follows: "ARTICLE 124: In order to ensure to citizen's freedom of conscience, the church in the U.S.S.R. is separated from the State, and the school from the church."[130] The separation of Church and State, as it is being enforced by modern judicial tyrants, is an un-American, communist doctrine.

In response to the school prayer decision, Roman Catholic clergy were adamant in their criticism of the Court. Cardinal Spellman stated that he was "shocked." Cardinal McIntyre viewed the holding as "scandalizing" and one that "puts shame on our faces as we are forced to emulate [Soviet Premier] Mr. Khrushchev." Americans characterized the decision as a "stupid... doctrinaire decision, an unrealistic decision, a decision that spits in the face of our history, our tradition, and our heritage as a religious people." In 1961, during a speech given at Wayne University, Herbert Aptheker, the editor of the communist monthly Political Affairs, is quoted as saying, "Neglect of parents to

---

[129]Matthew 15:3-9 NKJV

[130]*1936 Constitution of the USSR*, 1936, Bucknell, http://www.departments. bucknell.edu/russian/const/1936toc.html

teach our youth Christianity and Americanism has made the communist talk of deceiving American youth much easier."[131]

In seeking to remove Christianity from the public sphere, the U.S. government has now become a humanistic, and even communist, state wrapped in an American flag as a façade. The state has replaced God as the supreme law-giver, and Darwin has replaced Him as the Creator. Much of the blame can be laid at the feet of parents and school districts, who allowed their children to sit under the unconstitutional yoke of federal tyranny. Of course, these exclusions of religion only include Christianity. Thanks to the implementation of Common Core curriculum standards, Islam is now being taught in the Public Schools. In an article by Gina Cassini of Top Right News, we read:

> A father in Seminole County, Florida, is stunned after discovering an indoctrination "lesson" on Islam in his son's 10th-grade history textbook, a book that is also used as part of the Common Core standards across the state. Ron Wagner, who said he admittedly doesn't normally pay as much attention to his son's school assignments as he should, just happened to read from his son's world history book a statement which read, "There is no god, but God. Muhammad is the messenger of God." Wagner found out that his son is being indoctrinated in the religion of Islam in his 10th grade class from a history book used in school districts across the State of Florida. "Students were instructed to recite this prayer as the first Pillar of Islam, off of the board at the teacher's instruction," Mr. Wagner, who says he himself is not religious, told WFTV. Wagner, with a little further investigation, found out that his son was given an "Islam packet" and was even required to make an Islamic prayer rug for the world history class.[132]

---

[131]Billy James Hargis, *The Far Left*, Christian Crusade, 1964, p. 255.

[132]Gina Cassini, "Common Core School Assignment FORCES Students to Make Islamic Prayer Rugs, Recite Muslim Prayers," *Top Right News,* March 20, 2015,

Now, consider this scenario. Allegedly, during the recent Muslim holy month of Ramadan, teachers in Metro Nashville schools were actually ordered to release Muslim students from class at certain times – to go to unused classrooms or offices – so that they could attend to their Muslim prayers. A school spokesman says that, because the prayers are supposed to be uttered at designated times, that makes Muslim prayers different from Christian prayers. As a result, the school system tries to accommodate their religious traditions. One teacher told me, if she released her students from class for Christian prayers, she fears that she'd find herself in court. She does not think that is fair.

The excuse given by the school that, "because the prayers are supposed to be uttered at designated times, that makes Muslim prayers different from Christian prayers," is patently ridiculous. Christians are told to "pray without ceasing."[133]

We should not need permission from government bureaucrats, nor should we need to execute an appeals process, to exercise rights that were given by the Creator and protected by the Constitution. When the courts forbid us from praying in school, our response should be: "By what authority are you telling me what I can and cannot say? And who gave you this authority?" In response, there is no answer that they could give that is constitutional. Our response should then be: "The command to pray without ceasing and the protection granted by the First Amendment is all the permission I need to pray when I want, where I want, and to whom I want. I do not need official permission to do so!"

When the civil authorities overstep their authority and forbid what God has commanded, it is the duty of the people to defy them. In practice, the response of the American people should be: "Our right to pray comes from God! The Constitution does not forbid me to pray. *The constitution forbids you from telling me that I cannot pray!* Moreover, by doing so, you have become the Constitutional

---

http://toprightnews.com/common-core-school-assignment-forces-students-to-make-islamic-prayer-rug-recite-islamic-prayers/

[133] 1 Thessalonians 5:17 NKJV

lawbreaker. Therefore, your edicts carry no moral, legal, or constitutional authority, and God Himself does not require us to obey."

There has never been a law that makes prayer in school illegal. There cannot be. Such a law would violate the Constitution. Yet, Christians have been arrested and jailed for simply exercising their rights. When government officials fine or jail citizens without cause, this is tyranny! I challenge any judge or politician to demonstrate where "We the people" have granted the *authority* to regulate the religious lives of the American people. To regulate or restrict my religious freedom is the very definition of tyranny.

The Religious Oppression and Tyranny Continues

"Our Republic was formed on the basis that freedom is not a gift from government, but that freedom is a gift from God ... Among those freedoms is the right to worship according to our own beliefs. That is why I will get rid of, and totally destroy the Johnson Amendment and allow our representatives of faith to speak freely and without fear of retribution. I will do that – Remember."

— President Donald J. Trump
2017 National Prayer Breakfast Speech

In a speech at the Ohio State University, President Obama downplayed the claim that the government is tyrannical and is somehow responsible for many of America's problems. *"Still, you'll hear voices that incessantly warn of government as nothing more than some separate, sinister entity that's the root of all our problems, even as they do their best to gum up the works; or that tyranny always lurks just around the corner. You should reject these voices."[134]*

So should we follow his advice? Or does the evidence show that the federal government has increasingly and incrementally

---

[134]Barack Obama, "Commencement Address," (Speech, Columbus, May, 5, 2013) The Ohio State University, https://www.osu.edu/index.php?q=features/2013/obamacommencement.html

suppressed our rights? I argue in favor of the latter assertion, and submit the following example as proof.

Internal Revenue Service

One of the most glaring examples of tyranny is the suppression of our freedoms of religion and speech by the Internal Revenue Service (IRS). Acting like both a legislative and executive body, the IRS has passed laws and has even attempted to enforce them. Unfortunately, some Christian organizations, ignorant of the source of their rights, are strengthening the hand of these wrongdoers.

Consider the Christian Coalition of America, which claims to defend America's Godly heritage, but is actually guilty of silencing Christian pastors. The group's website instructs churches and pastors not to endorse or oppose candidates. It states the following:

What Churches May NOT Do:[135]
- Endorse candidates directly or indirectly on behalf of the church.
- Contribute funds or services (such as mailing lists or office equipment) directly to candidates or political committees.
- Distribute materials that clearly favor any candidate or party.
- Pay fees for partisan political events from church funds.
- Allow candidates to solicit funds while speaking in church.
- Set up a political committee that would contribute to candidates.

The Christian Coalition is clearly following what is called the "Johnson Amendment." In 1954, then-Senator Lyndon B. Johnson (D-Texas), recommended regulations for the IRS that bans pastors and churches from either endorsing or opposing political candidates. However, Congress has no authority to place these restrictions on the American church. In light of this fact, I have personally written the Christian Coalition on several occasions asking them, "By

---

[135]"DO's and DON'Ts for Churches," Christian Coalition, 2016, http://www.cc.org/church_liaisons

what authority has the IRS made these rules and who gave them the authority do so?" I have never received a response.

To place this critique in its proper context, allow me to use the following illustration. As a police officer, I was considered a "civil authority." While operating under the authority of law, I had a tremendous amount of power granted to me. I was even permitted to enter a house without a search warrant if I believed that a crime had been committed. However, my authority was still limited by the law and the Constitution. For me to search private property arbitrarily, just because I felt so inclined, would have been a violation of this same authority, since citizens have rights against illegal search and seizure as protected by the Fourth Amendment.

Government officials have restrictions placed on them by the Constitution. I may approach your house and demand to search it without actually having the authority to do so. As an American Citizen, whose rights are God-given and constitutionally protected, your response should be: "By what authority are you attempting to search my house and who gave you this authority?" This would require me to defend my course of action before beginning the search. This is because government officials cannot simply do whatever they want, whenever they want.

However, if I was a wicked individual and chaffed at the restrictions established by the Constitution, I might find a loophole to search your house without a warrant. I could, for instance, deputize another individual and say to them, "I do not have the authority to search this house without a warrant. So I will deputize you and have you search the house in my stead." Do you see the problem? The deputy receives his authority from me and I receive my authority (or lack of authority) from the Constitution. If it is illegal for me to search your house without a warrant, then it would be equally illegal for someone else (a deputy), who has received their authority from me, to legally search your premises.

Now let us apply this scenario to the IRS. The IRS works under the authority of Congress. It has essentially been deputized to collect taxes for the federal government. However, all government officials, including Congress, have restrictions placed on them by the Constitution. Freedom of religion and freedom of speech are both protected by the First Amendment: "Congress shall make no law respecting an establishment of religion, or *prohibiting the free exercise thereof; or abridging the freedom of speech*." Therefore, if it is illegal for Congress to pass any such laws, then the IRS, which receives its authority from Congress, is likewise prohibited from enacting the same.

Congressman Walter Jones of North Carolina recently introduced a bill called "Houses of Worship Free Speech Restoration Act." This bill would "restore the ability of churches and other houses of worship to participate more openly in the political process."[136] According to Congressman Jones:

> In 1954, then-Senator Lyndon B. Johnson offered an amendment to a revenue bill that would permanently extend the stranglehold of the Internal Revenue Service (IRS) into our nation's churches, synagogues and mosques. Since that time, the IRS has turned the 501(c)3 code-section on its head in an attempt to punish pastors, priests and rabbis for nothing more than communicating the principles of faith during an election period. If passed, the Houses of Worship Political Speech Protection Act would restore the rights of all religious organizations to determine for themselves what they can and cannot teach from their pulpits, or communicate to their congregation and the public without fear that their tax status may be in jeopardy... It is time to restore freedom to our Nation's pulpits.

While this attempt is nothing short of noble, it is totally unnecessary. There is no need to repeal the Johnson Amendment. It is an unjust law, and therefore "not a law," since it violates the First Amendment to the Constitution. We do not need to wait for Congress

---

[136]Walter B. Jones Jr, H.R.235 *Houses of Worship Free Speech Restoration Act*, 108th Congress, Library of Congress, https://www.congress.gov/bill/108th-congress/house-bill/235

to repeal the statute, and need not wait for the SCOTUS to declare it unconstitutional. It was unconstitutional the minute it was enacted!

The American Church need not wait for permission from government bureaucrats, nor must it engage in a long and costly judicial appeal process to exercise rights that were given by the Creator and protected by the Constitution. When the IRS says, "You cannot say that!" our response should be: "By what authority are you telling me what I can and cannot say? And who gave you this authority?" There is no answer they can give that is constitutional. Our response should then be: "The First Amendment is all the permission I need to say what I want, when I want! Moreover, I can endorse or denounce any political candidate that I choose. I do not need permission to do so!"

I challenge any judge or politician to demonstrate where "We the people" have granted the *authority* to regulate our religious practices or our right to free speech. To use the power of government (police, military or the courts) to enforce such unlawful edicts is the very definition of tyranny.

Historical Examples of Civil Disobedience

How Have Past Generations Dealt with Tyranny?

"Whether it is right in the sight of God to listen to you more than to God, you judge…. We ought to obey God rather than men!"[137]

~ Acts 4:16 & Acts 5:29

Many Christians view a civil rights movement as merely political. It is not! It is spiritual! It is a restoration of our American heritage, a heritage that acknowledges the LORD as our King, our Lawgiver, and our Judge.[138] This is the last, best and only chance that we have to save our American Republic from the deceitful plotting of wicked and unjust men.

Historically, in order for tyrants to gain total dictatorial control over an entire nation, they must accomplish either one of two agendas, or both. They must:

1. Deny the existence of the one true God, replacing Him with as supreme authority over all matters of law and justice. This has taken many forms throughout world history. In antiquity, the

---

[137]Acts 4:16, Acts 5:29 NKJV

[138]Isaiah 33:22 NKJV

Egyptian Pharaohs and the Roman Emperors would declare themselves to be gods on earth and claimed to be supreme over all matters. The modern U.S. equivalency would be the federal government, through illegal Supreme Court mandates, removing overt references to the true Creator from school textbooks and public life, thus declaring themselves to be supreme.

2. If they are dealing with a religious people, whom they cannot dissuade of God's existence, then they must distort Scripture to convince them that God requires blind and absolute obedience to the civil authorities.

Here is the contradiction that the Federal government has created for itself. The Federal Courts have already removed God as the supreme authority, as our nation has secularized itself. Now, these same tyrants are attempting to use the authority of Scripture to "preach" obedience to these same tyrants. Consider the following story reported by KLSA 12 out of Shreveport, Los Angeles.

In a news article titled *Homeland Security Enlist Clergy to Quell Public Unrest if Martial Law Ever Declared*, we learn that the federal government is presently enlisting Christian pastors to encourage popular compliance should the Constitution be "temporarily" suspended in a time of national emergency.

> Such clergy response teams would walk a tightrope during martial law between the demands of the government on the one side, versus the wishes of the public on the other. "In a lot of cases, these clergy would already be known in the neighborhoods in which they're helping to diffuse that situation," assured Sandy Davis. He serves as the director of the Caddo-Bossier Office of Homeland Security and Emergency Preparedness. For the clergy team, one of the biggest tools that they will have in helping calm the public down or to obey the law is the bible itself, specifically Romans 13. Dr. Tuberville elaborated, "Because the government's established by the

Lord, you know. And, that's what we believe in the Christian faith. That's what's stated in the scripture."[139]

How is it, that the federal government can force a faulty interpretation of the First Amendment, and the supposed separation of church and state, in order to convince the American people that the government is prohibited from endorsing religion, while attempting to use the authority of scripture found in Romans 13 to mandate blind obedience to the very same tyrants?

How is it that the federal government can indoctrinate children, against the wishes of their parents, in the unscientific teaching of evolution, which categorically denies the existence of a Creator, but then appeal to Scripture when it fits their purposes? Washington, we have a problem.

The answer is clear. The only use our federal officials have for sacred Scripture is as a propaganda tool that is used to control the populace. These wicked and unjust men have made themselves the enemy of God, aggressively attempting to remove Him as the supreme authority. And now they want "Christian" pastors to preach submission to this unconstitutional and illegitimate government? For the last 60 years, the U.S. Supreme Court has imposed an agenda that is anti-family, anti-Christian and anti-God, but that is also pro-evolution, pro-abortion, pro-pornography, pro-prostitution, pro-euthanasia, pro-homosexuality, and pro-humanism. And now, despite all this, they want to use clergy members to preach obedience to government tyrants rather than obedience to God? This would be like a man committing adultery with your wife and convincing her to leave you, and then having the gall to ask you to be the best man in their wedding. This is what many pastors and Christian leaders (clergy response teams) are being asked and convinced to do. What poor ignorant fools.

---

[139]Jeff Ferrell, "Homeland Security Enlists Clergy to Quell Public Unrest if Martial Law Ever Declared," *KSLA News*, March 22, 2012, http://www.ksla.com/story/6937987/homeland-security-enlists-clergy-to-quell-public-unrest-if-martial-law-ever-declared

The only recourse for the God-fearing, patriotic, American people is two-fold: to defy immoral and unconstitutional rulings (civil disobedience), and to "appeal" above their head (Appeal to Heaven).

Civil Disobedience

In an article published in the NY Daily news, a Fairleigh Dickinson University poll found that nearly half of all Republicans surveyed said they believed "an armed revolution in order to protect liberties might be necessary in the next few years." The "Appeal to Heaven" project hopes to use *non-violent* civil disobedience as a means of raising public awareness of the growing crisis in American.

Civil disobedience refers to the active refusal by the people of a nation to obey government laws, court rulings, directives, or presidential orders, *without resorting to physical violence.* It is the last hope to end an ever-festering conflict before it results in all out civil war, or the slaughter of millions of people. It is, moreover, an intentional and premeditated defiance of an established authority, whether that authority be religious, secular, or political. Yet, sadly, a large majority of Christian leaders in America believe that God condemns all types of civil disobedience. Others believe it to be so rarely permissible that they relegate it to a "non-option" status.

As we have discussed, tyrants have used a distorted interpretation of Romans 13, along with other scriptures, to compel the populace into acts of disobedience. The Apostle Paul warned us about ignorant men twisting Scripture to further their own agendas.[140] Unfortunately, today's equally biblically ignorant men and woman likewise do this to their own destruction.

The distorted use of these scriptures can seduce a biblically illiterate people into thinking God requires blind obedience to illegitimate government officials. HE DOES NOT! It is a proven biblical and historical fact that God DOES NOT require obedience to government officials who have removed themselves from the divine chain-of-command and who themselves do not submit to the doctrine of

---

[140]2 Peter 3:16 NKJV

higher authority. In fact, in such dire circumstances, *God actually requires disobedience.*

The biblical doctrine of civil disobedience stems from the biblical worldview that there is a "King of kings", a "LORD of lords", and a "Judge of judges" and that all people, at every time and in all nations, are bound by this truth. Individuals, nations, and leaders accept or reject this fact at their own peril.[141]

As discussed earlier, a catch-22 is a paradoxical situation in which a subordinate faces a set of contradictory rules or orders issued by superiors. God's people have been placed in a "no-win situation," forced to choose between disobeying God and disobeying our contemporary tyrants. This Dilemma is inevitable and there is no way around it! The question, then, is whom do we fear more? The answer should be clear.

> "And I say to you, my friends, do not be afraid of those who kill the body, and after that have no more that they can do. But I will show you whom you should fear: Fear Him who, after He has killed, has power to cast into hell; yes, I say to you, fear Him!"[142]

Each believer must choose for him or herself: Are you going to join the worldwide rebellion against God, or are you going to rebel against the unjust and illegal rulings of man? I do not know how any pastor or Christian theologian can read the whole of biblical and human history and cite one time where God's people were commended for obeying a tyrant rather than obeying God. A truly faithful people or nation says, "I am going to obey God rather than man at all costs." It is our *duty* as people of faith to defy unlawful edicts.

Hebrew Midwives – During Israel's' captivity in Egypt, the Egyptian king, Pharaoh, commanded that the midwives put to death the Hebrew children. "Then the king of Egypt spoke to the Hebrew midwives... and he said, 'When you do the duties of a midwife for the Hebrew

---

[141]Ps 33:12, Ps 2:1-6 NKJV

[142]Luke 12:4-5 NKJV

women, and see them on the birth stools, if it is a son, then you shall kill him; but if it is a daughter, then she shall live.' However, the midwives feared God, **and did not do as the king of Egypt commanded them**, but saved the male children alive. Therefore, God dealt well with the midwives, and the people multiplied and grew very mighty. And so it was, because the midwives feared God, that He provided households for them."[143]

The midwives, fearing God more than man, committed acts of civil disobedience of a governmental decree, by refusing to comply with this unjust law.

Shadrach, Meshach, and Abednego–During Israel's captivity in Babylon, the children of Israel were placed under the authority of King Nebuchadnezzar. It was the LORD that gave Nebuchadnezzar his kingdom and placed him in a position of authority. Daniel tells him so: "You, O king, are a king of kings. For the God of heaven has given you a kingdom, power, strength, and glory; and wherever the children of men dwell, or the beasts of the field and the birds of the heaven, He has given them into your hand, and has made you ruler over them all — you are this head of gold."[144]

Yet, while King Nebuchadnezzar was **"a"** king of kings, he was not **"the"** King of Kings! *His authority was a delegated authority*. He still had to answer to God for his every action, a fact that he lost sight of and chose to ignore. During his reign, he commanded all persons under his authority to worship his god and the statue of himself, or be thrown into a burning furnace. This was a violation of divine law and an act of tyranny. When the three Hebrew children, Shadrach, Meshach, and Abednego, learned of the law, they refused to comply, sighting the doctrine of higher authority. They reminded themselves of the first two of God's commandments: "You shall have no other gods before Me," and "You shall not make for yourself a carved image and you shall not bow down to them."[145] Nebuchadnezzar was playing the tyrant, as he was forcing, by law, his subjects into an act

---

[143]Ex 1:15-21 NKJV

[144]Dan 2:37-39 NKJV

[145]Ex. 20: 3-4 NKJV

of disobedience against God. Shadrach, Meshach, and Abednego answered and said to the king, "O Nebuchadnezzar, we have no need to answer you in this matter. If that is the case, our God whom we serve is able to deliver us from the burning fiery furnace, and He will deliver us from your hand, O king. But if not, let it be known to you, O king, that we do not serve your gods, nor will we worship the gold image which you have set up."[146]

In effect, the three Hebrew children said to the king, "Let us make this very clear to you. You have no authority to command us to violate a divine law. You are overstepping your authority in ordering us to defy God's commandments. The ball is now in your court! You do whatever it is you feel you need to do from this point on, but we will not comply with your orders because they are not lawful."

From God's perspective, the refusal of the three Hebrew children to comply with an unjust law was an act of faith and obedience to God. From the perspective of Nebuchadnezzar, this was an act of civil disobedience to the government official.

As you can imagine, people in authority do not like being disobeyed by their subordinates, even when it's the right course of action. In such circumstances, those in power will feel threatened and will choose to "push back." They may retaliate in either an aggressive or a passive aggressive way. In the case of King Nebuchadnezzar, he was "full of fury, and the expression on his face changed toward Shadrach, Meshach, and Abed-nego. He spoke and commanded that they heat the furnace seven times more than it was usually heated. And he commanded certain mighty men of valor who were in his army to bind Shadrach, Meshach, and Abed-nego, and cast them into the burning fiery furnace."[147]

King Nebuchadnezzar would eventually acknowledge his place in the universal chain-of-command and comply with the doctrine of higher authority. As a result, God was glorified by the obedience of His faithful servants and their disobedience to the tyrant. King Nebuchadnezzar would later proclaim: 'Blessed be the God of Shadrach, Meshach, and Abednego, who sent His Angel and

---

[146]Dan 3:16-18 NKJV

[147]Dan 3:19-21 NKJV

delivered His servants who trusted in Him, and they have frustrated the king's word, and yielded their bodies, that they should not serve nor worship any god except their own God! Therefore, I make a decree that any people, nation, or language which speaks anything amiss against the God of Shadrach, Meshach, and Abednego shall be cut in pieces, and their houses shall be made an ash heap; because there is no other God who can deliver like this.'[148]

Daniel–King Darius was convinced (tricked) by wicked government officials to sign a decree making it illegal to pray to God for a period of 30 days, in order to use the laws of government to put Daniel to death. We read: "All the governors of the kingdom, the administrators and satraps, the counselors and advisors, have consulted together to establish a royal statute and to make a firm decree, that whoever petitions any god or man for thirty days, except you, O king, shall be cast into the den of lions."[149]

Scripture is clear that Daniels' response was a willful and intentional act of civil disobedience. *"**Now when Daniel knew that the writing (law) was signed**, he went home. And in his upper room, with his windows open toward Jerusalem, he knelt down on his knees three times that day, and prayed and gave thanks before his God, as was his custom since early days."* (Dan 6:10)

After learning of the law, Daniel refused to comply, sighting the doctrine of higher authority. He asked himself, "Who is the highest authority that has ruled on this issue?" Since the right to pray was (and is) a right given to mankind by God, it becomes an inalienable right–that is, it cannot not be taken or suppressed by mortal powers... even government leaders.

Passing this law was an act of tyranny. Darius was using his power to compel his subjects to disobey God. Government leaders have no authority to forbid people from praying. This is a right that has been bestowed by our Creator, and the refusal of Daniel to comply was an act of civil disobedience. He essentially said, "The ball is now

---

[148]Dan 3:28-29, Dan 4:34-37 NKJV

[149]Dan 6:7-8 NKJV

in your court! You do whatever it is you feel you need to do from this point on, but I will not comply with your order because it is not lawful." Again, God saved Daniel, and King Darius was reminded of his place in the divine chain-of-command. Again, God was glorified. Darius proclaimed: 'I make a decree that in every dominion of my kingdom men must tremble and fear before the God of Daniel. For He is the living God, and steadfast forever; His kingdom is the one which shall not be destroyed, and His dominion shall endure to the end. He delivers and rescues, And He works signs and wonders in heaven and on earth, who has delivered Daniel from the power of the lions.'[150]

The Apostles–In the Book of Acts, Peter and the other Apostles were jailed for preaching the gospel of Jesus Christ. After a time, they were released by the Jewish leaders and commanded not to preach in the name of Jesus any longer. Later, they were again brought before their leaders and were asked, "Did we not strictly command you not to teach in this name?" Yet the apostles asked themselves, "Who is the highest authority on this issue?" Since an angel of the LORD had commanded them to "go, stand in the temple and speak to the people all the words of this life...," Peter and the other apostles answered and said, "We ought to obey God rather than men."[151]

The refusal of the Apostles to comply with an unjust ruling by their highest court was an act of civil disobedience. They essentially said, "The ball is now in your court! You do whatever it is you feel you need to do from this point on, but we will not comply with your orders because they are not lawful." After some consultation, the Jewish leaders called for the Apostles, beat them and commanded that they should not speak in the name of Jesus, and they were released once again. Where did they go? Right back into the temple where "they did not cease teaching and preaching Jesus as the Christ."[152]

---

[150]Dan 6:26-27 NKJV

[151]Acts 5: 28-29 NKJV

[152]Acts 5:40-42 NKJV

In every one of these accounts, we can begin to see and apply this biblical directive. Whenever government leaders take themselves out from under the divine chain-of-command and use force, intimidation, or threats to make God's people violate the divine order, then it *is the right and the duty* of mankind to obey God, rather than the civil authority. Therefore, in such instances, disobeying tyrannical edicts is, in fact, an act of obedience to God. This truth would be sublimely practiced and articulated by America's Founding Fathers.

Contemporary Examples of Civil Disobedience

How Have Americans Dealt with Tyranny?

"Rebellion to Tyrants is Obedience to God." [153]

~ Benjamin Franklin

Revolutionary War–Some theologians believe the American War for Independence was a violation of Romans 13. However, our Founding Fathers were following and advocating the doctrine of higher authority at the national level. While the stories from the last chapter were individual accounts of civil disobedience, the Declaration of Independence served as an act of civil disobedience at the national level by a people who were guided by a biblical worldview. To understand this, we must first understand the historical context of America's founding.

After the protestant Reformation, in which Martin Luther refused to comply with the laws of the Catholic Church, Christianity began to spread like wildfire throughout the European continent. However, much persecution followed from both protestant and Catholic leaders who felt their power slipping, as the people began to recognize a higher authority that first and foremost demanded their obedience.

---

[153] *PTJ*, The Source of "Rebellion to tyrants is obedience to God, *Bradshaw's Epitaph*, Appendix II, 1:677-79.

While this trend was actually occurring all over Europe, let us consider the situation as it existed in England.

Following the crowning of Charles II, church meeting-houses were closed. All English citizens were required by law to attend the (protestant) Anglican Church services, which taught the "divine right of Kings" from Romans 13, to solicit unwavering obedience to the monarchy. It became punishable by law to conduct any religious service, address a congregation, or even to hold a religious meeting without government approval. This is what is called "establishing religion by law." Passing these laws was an act of tyranny. Those who disagreed with the new law and the teaching of the Anglican Church were called "non-conformists", because they were preaching the real interpretation of Romans 13 – the doctrine of higher authority. The most famous of these non-conformists was a man named John Bunyan who, while imprisoned for violating the law, wrote *Pilgrims Progress*. Bunyan argued that God's word commanded him to "Preach the word!" both "in season and out of season."[154] Citing the doctrine of higher authority, he argued that the civil authorities had no right to pass laws restricting his preaching. Scripture did not say that men have to receive authority from, or be licensed by, government officials in order to preach God's word. The Sanhedrin also tried to pull this same trick on Jesus when they felt their power slipping away.[155]

Non-conformists, like Bunyan, began to circumvent these laws by holding "bible studies," and not actual "church services." In early 1664, the English Parliament passed the Conventicle Act, which made it illegal to hold "bible studies" of more than four people or to hold an unsanctioned church service. This dark period in English legal history, in which freedom of religion was greatly curtailed, motivated most of the early American colonists (starting with the Pilgrims) to flee the persecutions of "Christian" Europe and sail to the New World. By the time the wheels were in motion that led to the writing of the Declaration of Independence, the vast majority of the American people believed that God had led Christopher Columbus to discover the New World, even though it was 25 years before the

---

[154]2 Tim 4:2 NKJV

[155]Matt 21:23, Mark 11:27 NKJV

Protestant Reformation. It was always meant to be a place of sanctuary for the persecuted Christians of Europe. This belief was articulated by Thomas Paine in his revolutionary pamphlet *Common Sense*, which was written in 1775 and was the best-selling book (other than the Bible) in American history at the time. Paine's writings inspired and convinced the American Christian colonists to declare independence from Great Britain in the summer of 1776. In his pamphlet, he wrote, "The Reformation was preceded by the discovery of America: As if the Almighty graciously meant to open a sanctuary to the persecuted [Christians] in future years, when home should afford neither friendship nor safety."[156]

Some Christian refugees in the New World believed that monarchy was, and is, a "sin", as it usurps the divine prerogative of Heaven and places man at the top of the divine chain-of-command. Thomas Paine again wrote: "Government by kings was first introduced into the world by the Heathens, from whom the children of Israel copied the custom. It was the most prosperous invention the Devil ever set on foot for the promotion of idolatry. The Heathens paid divine honours to their deceased kings, and the *Christian World* hath improved on the plan by doing the same to their living ones...."[157]

The early American colonists wanted to follow the example of ancient Israel and establish a government that recognized and enshrined the doctrine of higher authority in its very structure. They even believed that ancient Israel, though essentially theocratic, was actually a de facto Republic— in which all people were afforded equal protection under the law and only the LORD Himself was considered King. To be clear, the Founding Fathers did not believe in "Utopias" (societies possessing near perfect qualities), but they did believe that when nations followed the divine order, they would be creating the most perfect government that is humanly possible. Seven years before the Declaration of Independence, John Adams would

---

[156]Thomas Paine, *Common Sense,* Essay, January 9, 1776, Source: Bill of Rights Institute, https://billofrightsinstitute.org/founding-documents/primary-source-documents/common-sense/

[157]Thomas Paine, *Common Sense,* Essay, January 9, 1776, Source: Bill of Rights Institute, https://billofrightsinstitute.org/founding-documents/primary-source-documents/common-sense/

write: "Human Government is more or less perfect, as it approaches nearer or diverges farther from an Imitation of this perfect Plan of divine and moral Government."[158]

Thomas Paine, in his revolutionary pamphlet *Common Sense,*, drew from the Books of Judges and 1st Samuel to make his case for rejecting the monarchy and establishing an American Republic based upon the model of Israel:

> Near three thousand years passed away, from the Mosaic account of the creation, till the Jews under a national delusion requested a king. Till then their form of government (except in extraordinary cases where the Almighty interposed) was a kind of Republic, administered by a judge and the elders of the tribes. Kings they had none, and it was held sinful to acknowledge any being under that title but the Lord of Hosts. And when a man seriously reflects on the idolatrous homage which is paid to the persons of kings, he need not wonder that the Almighty, ever jealous of his honour, should disapprove a form of government which so impiously invades the prerogative of Heaven. Monarchy is ranked in scripture as one of the sins of the Jews, for which a curse in reserve is denounced against them... These portions of scripture are direct and positive. They admit of no equivocal construction. That the Almighty hath here entered his protest against monarchical government is true, or the scripture is false.[159]

There has been a considerable effort by secularists to whitewash American history of its biblical influence, when it was the Founders'

---

[158]"Draft of a Newspaper Communication," The Adams Papers, 2016, https://www.masshist.org/publications/apde2/view?id= ADMS-01-01-02-0014-0005-0005

[159]Thomas Paine, *Common Sense,* Essay, January 9, 1776, Source: Bill of Rights Institute, https://billofrightsinstitute.org/founding-documents/ primary-source-documents/common-sense/

appeal to Romans chapter 13 that gave their cause moral and legal legitimacy. They did not want trouble with the civil authorities, which is the reason they left Europe, but the formidable shadow of the English government followed them to the New World and imposed laws that threatened to deprive them of their God-given rights. The colonists were forced into a no-win, or catch 22, situation. Their backs were to the wall and there was no place left to go. This is where they would have to make their stand!

The straw that seems to have "broke the camel's back" was Parliament's passing of the American Colonies Act of 1766. Also known as the Declaratory Act, it was a declaration of the King's and Parliament's unlimited authority over the American colonies. The colonists were "bound to obey every law" passed by the British government–even those laws that superseded the divine order and restricted their religious freedoms–and that the crown was justified in using government to enforce compliance. *The colonists saw this as nothing less than government imposed slavery!* In his next political writing titled *The Crisis,* which was written six months after the Declaration of Independence, Thomas Paine exposed the arrogance of a government administration that had become so drunk with power that it sought to replace God Himself. "Britain, with an army to enforce her tyranny, has declared that she has a right (not only to TAX) but 'to BIND us in ALL CASES WHATSOEVER' and if being bound in that manner, is not slavery, then is there not such a thing as slavery upon earth. Even the expression is impious; for so unlimited a power can belong only to God."[160]

The colonists felt that the British government was usurping the authority of heaven just as Pharaoh, Nebuchadnezzar and King Darius had done in ages past. After *years* of appealing to the British government, they were left in a no-win, or 'catch 22 situation.' They could either disobey God or disobey the tyrant. Therefore, with their backs to the wall, they were left with no choice but to either submit to government imposed slavery or:

1. Defy their immoral rulings. (Civil disobedience) and
2. "Appeal" above the king's head. (Appeal to Heaven)

---

[160]Thomas Paine, *The Crisis* (London: R. Carlisle, 1819)

The Founding Fathers' understanding of biblical, civil disobedience at the national level can be seen in the Declaration of Independence, when they declared that they were *"opposing with manly firmness* his invasions on the (God-given) rights of the people." And that, furthermore, they were "appealing to the Supreme Judge of the world for the [righteousness] of our intentions" and "with a firm reliance on the protection of divine Providence." The Declaration of Independence let the king know which choice they had made. They essentially said: "Let us make this very clear to you. You have no authority to command us to violate a divine law. The ball is now in your court! You do whatever it is you feel you need to do from this point on, but we will not comply with your orders because they are not lawful."

The Declaration of Independence was not a declaration of war. It was a statement of faith and a declaration of God-given rights. As you can imagine, people in authority do not like when their subordinates refuse to comply with their orders; even when the subordinates have taken the proper legal or divine position. Therefore, it is not unusual for those in power to "push back." Authorities that have forgotten, or do not wish to comply with the doctrine of higher authority because they have developed a power mad "god-complex", will oftentimes retaliate in either an aggressive or passive aggressive way.

In the case of Britain, the response was aggressive. Were the colonists wrong for demanding the separation? Were the colonists wrong for defending themselves? *No!* People have a right to defend themselves against criminal injustice and violence, even at the government level. Even Jesus commanded his disciples to carry swords on some of their journeys.[161] Jesus understood the dangers that were faced by travelers who journeyed between towns (i.e. the story of the Good Samaritan.). Man has always retained the right to "defend" himself lawfully against wicked and unjust men. While we are told to "turn the other cheek," nowhere in scripture are we commanded to allow government lawbreakers to murder us or steal our property. On the other hand, the scriptures do not allow for grossly provocative

---

[161]Luke 22:36 NKJV

or offensive wars on a nation or an individual. With this biblical understanding, Thomas Paine again defends the colonist's decision:

> Not all the treasures of the world, so far as I believe, could have induced me to support an offensive war, for I think it murder; but if a thief breaks into my house, burns and destroys my property, and kills or threatens to kill me, or those that are in it, and to *'bind me in all cases whatsoever'* to his absolute will, am I to suffer it? What signifies it to me, whether he who does it is a king or a common man; my countryman or not my countryman; whether it be done by an individual villain, or an army of them? If we reason to the root of things we shall find no difference; neither can any just cause be assigned why we should punish in the one case and pardon in the other.[162]

To justify their civil disobedience, one of the Founding Fathers' favorite mottos was "disobedience to tyrants is obedience to God." On the same day that the Declaration of Independence was signed (July 4, 1776), the Continental Congress created a committee and designed a Great Seal for the new nation. The committee consisted of three of America's most prominent Founding Fathers: Benjamin Franklin, Thomas Jefferson, and John Adams. Their suggestions again demonstrate the biblical influence underpinning their cause.

Benjamin Franklin chose an allegorical scene from Exodus, described in his notes as 'Moses standing on the Shore, and extending his Hand over the Sea, thereby causing the same to overwhelm Pharaoh who is sitting in an open Chariot, a Crown on his Head and a Sword in his Hand. Rays from a Pillar of Fire in the Clouds reaching to Moses, to express that he acts by Command of the Deity.' Motto,

---

[162]Thomas Paine, *The Crisis* (London: R. Carlisle, 1819)

'Rebellion to Tyrants is Obedience to God.' Jefferson suggested a depiction of the Children of Israel in the wilderness, led by a cloud by day and a pillar of fire by night for the front of the seal.[163]

As can be seen by the outcome of this congressional committee, many of the Founding Fathers were highly influenced by the story of the Exodus. Today's secular humanists and historical revisionists would have considered this a violation of the fictitious separation of church and state.

This type of biblical influence did not originate in America. Following the Protestant Reformation, men such as Theodore Beza, a French theologian, and John Knox, a Scottish clergyman and the founder of the Presbyterian denomination in Scotland, taught that Christians have not only the right to oppose a tyrannical government, but in many cases the duty as well. Benjamin Franklin and Thomas Jefferson's use of the phrase "disobedience to tyrants is obedience to God" can be traced to a quote by John Knox from the year 1558: "Obedience to God's laws by disobeying man's wicked laws is very commendable. But to disobey God for any duty to man is all together damnable."[164]

Thomas Jefferson is also quoted as saying, "When injustice becomes law then resistance becomes duty."[165] What did he mean? Injustice by definition is a violation of God's law and/or a violation of another person's God-given rights. Whenever the civil authorities pass laws that either violate rights or compel disobedience to divine law, then the right to rebel is authorized by heaven.

However, one must be very careful with the idea of rebellion and revolution. Ultimately, one must ask: "What is the end game. What would a successful revolution look like?" Is it a revolution that seeks to restore divine order, the rightful King to His throne? Is it a revolution that seeks to displace the rightful King and replace him with a

---

[163]MacArthur, John D. "First Great Seal Committee – July/August 1776". Greatseal. com.

[164]David W. Hall, *The Genevan Reformation and the American Founding*, (Maryland, Lexington Books, 2003)

[165]"When injustice becomes law, resistance becomes duty", Monticello, http://www.monticello.org/site/research-and-collections/ when-injustice-becomes-law-resistance-becomes-duty-quotation

human counterfeit? The former has a proven track record of success and the latter a track record of failure. Consider two revolutions: The American and the French.

In the late 1700s, both the American and French Revolutions sought to remove the reign of their kings. The American sought to replace the British king with the King of Kings while the French sought to install man as the highest authority. The American Revolution sought to restore the divine order, as John Adams explained: "The highest, the transcendent glory of the American Revolution was this — it connected, in one indissoluble bond, the principles of civil government with the precepts of Christianity."[166] The result of this revolution was the establishment of the form of government that has existed, and succeeded, in America for nearly 200 years.

With the success of the American Revolution, the French also sought to overthrow their tyrant Louis XVI in 1789. Their new government would be grounded on reason (enlightenment) rather than on the laws of God. Thus, France erected a government that was purely secular. The results were grotesquely tragic. By 1796, the French Revolution had experienced the Reign of Terror in which over 40,000 Frenchmen were put to death. France then, essentially, became a military dictatorship under Napoleon. By April 1814, Napoleon was deposed and the French monarchy was restored as Louis XVIII, the younger brother of Louis XVI, became king.

Within a span of about 25 years, France had lost countless lives and ultimately ended up right where she started – ruled by a monarch. Why had the America Revolution succeeded and the French Revolution failed? This question so intrigued a young French political scientist named Alexis de Tocqueville, that he traveled to the United States to discover why the American Revolution had led to freedom, liberty, and prosperity, while the French Revolution led to a dictatorship, resulting in mass murder and terror. He published his finding in a two volume book titled *Democracy in America.*

His finding did not surprise those who understood divine order, which the Americans recognized and followed through their civil

---

[166]John Adams, "Letters Of President John Adams," *The Historical Magazine*, Vol. IV, July 1860, 193

government. *Now the Lord is the Spirit; and where the Spirit of the Lord is, there is liberty.*[167] France did not have the spirit. Alexis de Tocqueville: "The Americans combine the notions of Christianity and of liberty so intimately in their minds, that it is impossible to make them conceive the one without the other... In France I had almost always seen the spirit of religion and the spirit of freedom marching in opposite directions. But in America I found they were intimately united and that they reigned in common over the same country."[168]

The American Civil War–America experienced its greatest loss of life in the conflict known as The Civil War. This could have been prevented if the American church had understood, and applied, the doctrine of higher authority to settle the conflict before it became bloody. Before we address this subject, we must first seek to understand the historical context that led to the war. For those in the South, the war was about the States' right to own slaves. For the abolitionists in the North it was about eradicating slavery. (This topic is covered in greater detail in my book *The Rise of America: Fighting the Next American Revolution and the Constitutional Crisis*). The Christian church could, and should, have been able to settle this conflict before it festered into an all-out war by applying the doctrine of higher authority to the administration of civil government.

Let us briefly clear up some common misconceptions about slavery, as I have heard politicians criticize our good LORD by saying that He advocated slavery in the Old Testament. *This is categorically false.* In the Old Testament, there were two types of slavery – indentured servitude and forced servitude, or slavery. Indentured servitude was a voluntary labor system and permitted by God. Under Mosaic Law, kidnapping a person or even owning a kidnapped person was punishable by death. The Divine Law reads: "He who kidnaps a man and sells him, or if he is found in his hand, shall surely be put to death."[169] Forced servitude, or slavery, as it was being practiced

---

[167]2 Cor 3:17 NKJV

[168]Alexis de Tocqueville, *Democracy in America,* (Chicago: The University of Chicago Press, 2002)

[169]Ex 21:16 NKJV

in the American South, was illegal because it required kidnapping people and forcing them into involuntary or forced servitude. Under the slave system in the American South, a person was no longer owned by God, but by man. *He was property.* As property, the slave owner could do whatever seemed right in his eyes, including beating, raping, or killing the person. An indentured servant, however, could not be touched. If you so much as knocked out his tooth, he would be set free. "If a man strikes the eye of his male or female servant, and destroys it, he shall let him go free for the sake of his eye. And if he knocks out the tooth of his male or female servant, he shall let him go free for the sake of his tooth."[170]

Slavery did not come to America on the Mayflower. Slavery was imported by the British crown and aristocracy to all its colonies worldwide, including the American colonies. (Here I would highly recommend the movie *Amazing Grace*). Therefore, the type of slavery that was being practiced in America before the Civil War was an abomination to God and a tyrannical violation of divine law. Any act of civil disobedience, with regard to slavery, was biblically justifiable and approved by God, so long as the act was not itself a violation of divine law (i.e. murder, etc.).

The Christian abolitionists who ended slavery came from churches and religious denominations, such as the Religious Society of Friends (Quakers), Congregationalists, Wesleyans, and Reformed Presbyterians. They were also from breakaway sects of mainstream denominations such as branches of the Methodist church and American Baptists. They ended slavery by:

1. Defying unjust and illegal slavery laws. (Civil disobedience) and
2. "Appealing" above the head of the civil officials. (Appeal to Heaven)

The practice of civil disobedience can be seen in the formation of the Underground Railroad. The Underground Railroad was a series of secret routes that led to safe houses, which enabled escaped slaves

---

[170]Ex 21:26-27 NKJV

to travel to free states and Canada with the aid of the Christian abolitionists, who understood that "when injustice becomes law then resistance becomes duty."

Because of the successful efforts of the Christian abolitionists in leading slaves to freedom, the Federal Government passed the "Fugitive Slave Act". This made it a federal crime not to return a slave to his or her master. The Christian abolitionist, understanding the divine principle that "an unjust law is no law at all" if it violates the doctrine of higher authority, not only refused to return escaped slaves to their masters, but also funded their means of escape. Again the Divine Law reads: "You shall not give back to his master the slave who has escaped from his master to you. He may dwell with you in your midst, in the place which he chooses within one of your gates, where it seems best to him; *you shall not oppress him*."[171] This is what was commanded by heaven and the abolitionists believed that "we ought to obey God rather than men."[172]

This was not just practiced by a few radicals and non-conformists; it was practiced by entire states. In 1854, the Wisconsin Supreme Court declared the Fugitive Slave Act unconstitutional because it violated both the Tenth Amendment to the Constitution and The Doctrine of Higher Authority.[173] In 1850, the Vermont legislature passed a "Habeas Corpus Law," which required, by law, all Vermont judicial and law enforcement officials to assist captured fugitive slaves in finding their way to freedom.[174]

Martin Luther King Jr.–No man in modern history better understood how to apply civil disobedience and the doctrine of higher authority to a righteous cause than Martin Luther King Jr. (MLK).

---

[171]Deut 23:15-16 NKJV

[172]Acts 5:29 NKJV

[173]The Wisconsin Supreme Court declares the Fugitive Slave Act unconstitutional, Wisconsin Historical Society, https://www.wisconsinhistory.org/turningpoints/search.asp?id=170

[174]John R. McKivigan, *Abolitionism and American Law*, (Indianapolis: Garland Publishing, Inc., 1999) 326

His advocating of passive, non-violent resistance brought segregation and legalized state-sponsored racism to an end.

MLK understood, from history, that freedom is never voluntarily given by the oppressor; it must be demanded by the oppressed. His advocating of civil disobedience was a way of bringing public attention to the unjust laws that plagued the South. The worst of these were called the "Jim Crow Laws." The Jim Crow laws segregated most public places, including public schools and public transportation. They also called for the segregation of "whites only" and "blacks only" restaurants, restrooms, and drinking fountains. These laws were unconstitutional as they restricted the people's freedom of speech, freedom of the press, and made it illegal for any person to advocate equality between the races. In a pamphlet titled *"Laws Governing the Conduct of Nonwhites and Other Minorities"* we read: "Any person printing, publishing or circulating written matter urging for public acceptance of social equality between white and Negros, is subject to imprisonment."[175] In other words: "Anyone saying that whites and black are created equal in the eyes of God will go to jail!"

On April 12, 1963, eight white Alabama clergymen wrote an article titled "A Call for Unity," stirring up opposition against MLK's methods. MLK responded with his now famous *Letter from the Birmingham Jail*. The "writing, printing, publishing and circulating" of MLK's letter by other black pastors, in which he openly and defiantly calls for the Christian church to take up the cause of racial equality, was an act of civil disobedience as it defied the Jim Crow Laws.

In a scene reminiscent of the Sanhedrin asking Jesus "by what authority are You doing these things?"[176], MLK was asked by his fellow clergyman *by what authority* he defied unjust and immoral segregation laws. He responded that his "authority" came from a much higher office than any earthly court. Understanding the true meaning of Romans 13, he responded to this question put to him by fellow clergy members:

---

[175]"Jim Crow Laws," National Park Service, https://www.nps.gov/malu/learn/education/jim_crow_laws.htm

[176]Matt 21:23 NKJV

The answer lies in the fact that there are two types of laws: just and unjust. I would be the first to advocate obeying just laws. One has not only a legal but a moral responsibility to obey just laws. Conversely, one has a moral responsibility to disobey unjust laws. I would agree with St. Augustine that 'an unjust law is no law at all.' Now, what is the difference between the two? How does one determine whether a law is just or unjust? A just law is a man-made code that squares with the *moral law or the law of God*. An unjust law is a code that is out of harmony with the moral law. To put it in the terms of St. Thomas Aquinas: An unjust law is a human law that is not rooted in eternal law and natural law.[177]

He was also asked why he would choose direct actions of civil disobedience, (sit-ins, marches, etc.) as opposed to negotiation. MLK was not opposed to negotiation. The problem was that racists had decided the "case was closed" and there was no need for further negotiations. The purpose of direct action was to raise awareness, by creating a non-violent crisis and establishing enough tension to force communities to confront the issue. He needed to dramatize the problem, so that it could no longer be ignored. MLK summed up his case by appealing to both biblical and world history:

Of course, there is nothing new about this kind of civil disobedience. It was seen sublimely in the refusal of Shadrach, Meshach, and Abednego to obey the laws of Nebuchadnezzar because a higher moral law was involved. It was practiced superbly by the early Christians, who were willing to face hungry lions and the excruciating pain of chopping blocks before submitting to certain unjust laws of the Roman Empire... We can never forget that everything Hitler did in

---

[177]Martin Luther King Jr. *Letter From a Birmingham Jail,* April 16, 1963, African Studies Center, https://www.africa.upenn.edu/Articles_Gen/Letter_Birmingham.html

Germany was 'legal' and everything the Hungarian freedom fighters did in Hungary was 'illegal.' It was 'illegal' to aid and comfort a Jew in Hitler's Germany. But I am sure that if I had lived in Germany during that time, I would have aided and comforted my Jewish brothers even though it was illegal. If I lived in a Communist country today where certain principles dear to the Christian faith are suppressed, I believe I would openly advocate disobeying these anti-religious laws.[178]

Can we still look at the whole of biblical and American history and not see the divine directive? Throughout history, God fearing and bible believing Christians have been forced into a situation of civil disobedience or rebellion. Not rebellion to God, but rather rebellion to the unjust laws and rulings of tyrants. As Benjamin Franklin stated: 'Rebellion to Tyrants is Obedience to God.'

Whenever people of faith decided to obey God instead of man, regardless of the threat of punishment, they were highly favored by God and remembered throughout history as people of great faith and courage. When we read the "Hall of Fame of Faith" found in the book of Hebrews, we realize that "by faith" Daniel *stopped the mouths of lions*, and "by faith" the three Hebrew Children *quenched the violence of fire*.[179] I believe that "Hall of Fame of Faith" is still being written to this day. "By faith" the pilgrims held church services and bible studies in violation of the laws of England. "By faith" the Founding Fathers wrote the Declaration of Independence. "By faith" the Christian abolitionists harbored runaway slaves and established the Underground Railroad. "By faith" MLK staged "sit-ins" at white only restaurants and willfully violated Jim Crow laws in the 1960s. "By faith" Rosa Parks willfully violated a city law demanding she give up her bus seat to a white person. Unfortunately, the Christian

---

[178]Martin Luther King Jr. *Letter From a Birmingham Jail*, April 16, 1963, African Studies Center, https://www.africa.upenn.edu/Articles_Gen/Letter_ Birmingham.html

[179]Heb 11:33-34 NKJV

church in 21st century America appears to be nothing more than a faithless, empty shell of what it once was. As a result, it has become nothing more than an irrelevant social club. Maybe this is why Jesus wondered to Himself: "Nevertheless, when the Son of Man comes, will He really find faith on the earth?"[180]

The rise and fall of every great nation may be inevitable. However, the restoration of a nation is possible when people of faith are willing to have the courage to return the rightful King to his throne. The federal government has no moral or constitutional authority to deny the American people their right to acknowledge this truth, nor do they have the authority to deny the American people of their religious liberties! If those in government cannot find the moral courage to do what is right, then people of faith must obey God, rather than man, regardless of the consequences.

---

[180]Luke 18:8 NKJV

May I Approach the Bench?

Appealing to the Divine Judge

We, therefore, the Representatives of the United States of America, in General Congress, Assembled, appealing to the Supreme Judge of the world for the righteousness of our intentions.[181]

Declaration of Independence

Several years ago, when the LORD called me to begin the Appeal to Heaven project, I began to research the meaning and purpose of this phrase. Unfortunately, an internet search for *Appeal to Heaven* only returned vague historical references to a Revolutionary War flag. Most people have never heard the term and most do not even recognize that it was actually America's first flag. In the last couple of years, the LORD has supernaturally placed this phrase in the collective consciousness of those Christian and government leaders who have been diligently praying for the restoration of America.

After years of prayer from both intercessors and prophets alike, God has been prodding us in the right direction. YouTube videos on *Appeal to Heaven* by Dutch Sheets, Jennifer LeClaire or Gary Beaton give great insight on what God is starting to reveal to us. The release

---

[181]Thomas Jefferson, *The Declaration of Independence*, Essay, July 4th, 1776, http://teachingamericanhistory.org/library/document/declaration-of-independence/

of two recent books—*The Next Great Move of God–An Appeal to Heaven for Spiritual Awakening* by Jennifer LeClaire and, *An Appeal To Heaven: What Would Happen If We Did It Again* by Dutch Sheets—are two more examples of how God is beginning to reveal this concept to His saints as the only real solution for national restoration.

However, I believe that these insights are just the beginning and not the end. They are just the tip of the iceberg. Prophets and intercessors have brought us this far. I would suggest that teachers and theologians would take us the rest of the way. In order to bring about a national restoration, we must first understand exactly what the Appeal to Heaven principles are and then seek to apply them in a constructive manner.

Throughout history, Christian theologians have retained a sound formulation of the triune nature of God (Father, Son and Holy Spirit), but along the way, many of them have lost sight of His triune administrative duties over the nations as *our King, our Lawgiver, and Judge*.[182] This refers to Christ's' status as the Supreme head of the universal chain-of-command—as explained in Romans 13. Earlier in Scripture, Isaiah 9:6-7 teaches us:

> For unto us a Child is born, unto us a Son is given; and *the government will be upon His shoulder*. And His name will be called Wonderful, Counselor, Mighty God, Everlasting Father, Prince of Peace. *Of the increase of His government and peace There will be no end*, Upon the throne of David and over His kingdom, to order it and establish it with judgment and justice from that time forward, even forever. The zeal of the Lord of hosts will perform this.[183]

Many Christians have missed the importance of the chronological sequence of this passage, which refers to Christ's birth (a Child is born), His manhood (unto us a Son is given), and His kingship over the nations (the government will be upon His shoulder). The phrase *the*

---

[182]Isaiah 33:22 NKJV

[183]Isaiah 9:6-7 NKJV

government will be upon His shoulder is a reference to governmental authority. In the Old Testament, when a person was given supreme authority over the affairs of a nation, a key was laid upon their shoulder as was done to Eliakim the son of Hilkiah. "The key of the house of David I will lay on his shoulder."[184] These keys were given to Christ because he is the one "who has the key of David, He who opens and no one shuts, and shuts and no one opens."[185] These keys in turn have been entrusted to the Church: "And I will give you the keys of the kingdom of heaven, and whatever you bind on earth will be bound in heaven, and whatever you loose on earth will be loosed in heaven."[186]

In the fulfillment of His governmental and administrative duties over the nations, Christ can be said "to wear many hats." This phrase means that a person may have more than one set of responsibilities or hold more than one political office. The mayor can also be the police chief. A person may be both CEO and the chairman of the board.

In most modern legal systems, the power of government is usually spread among many people: lawmakers make the laws, judges decide questions of law, a jury hears the facts and decides a person's guilt or innocence, and the penal system enforces verdicts. This keeps one person from being judge, jury and executioner all at once— important because the greatest atrocities committed in history have been when one unjust man has been given all authority.

However, our LORD and KING Jesus Christ, who is perfectly righteous and just, has been given all authority over the nation of this world.[187] As our founding fathers understood, His laws are binding all over the globe, in all countries, and at all times. Christ explicitly taught, "All authority has been given to Me in heaven and on earth…" Therefore, according to Romans 13, Christ is the supreme heard of all human government. The Word *supreme* means: The Highest in authority; holding the highest place in government or power. Therefore, Christ reins not only in Heaven, but on Earth as

---

[184]Isaiah 22:20-22 NKJV

[185]Rev 3:7 NKJV

[186]Matt 16:19 NKJV

[187]Isaiah 11:4; 32:1 NKJV

the Supreme government official. Christ is our Supreme King, our Supreme Lawgiver, and Supreme Judge.[188]

After Christ claimed that He had been given supreme authority in heaven and on earth, He gave His disciples the "Great Commission" and instructed them to go and take this message to the all nations. Many theologians have confused Jesus' command to "preach the gospel to every creature," found in Mark 16:15-16, with His admonition to "teach them to observe all things that I have commanded," found in Matt 28:18-20.

Both gospel accounts record only a portion of what Christ taught. Thus, the fullness of our commission might read as follows: "Go into all the world and preach the gospel to every creature, making disciples of all the nations by baptizing them in the name of the Father and of the Son and of the Holy Spirit.... And then teach them to observe all things that I have commanded you; and lo, I am with you always, even to the end of the age."

The Great Commission must be viewed as a systematic three-fold process that encompasses the whole of Christianity. This process could be enumerated as 1) Preach the gospel to them (seek to convert every creature); 2) Baptize them (in the name of the Father, the Son and the Holy Spirit; 3) Disciple them by (teaching them to observe all things that I have commanded). Notice that the second command (to baptize new believers) is an enumeration on the first (to convert). The third command (to make disciples) must follow. It is not enough to convert someone to Christianity. The whole overall purpose of Christianity[189] is to disciple new converts[190] until they are systematically transformed and conformed into the image of Christ.[191]

Everyone who is perfectly trained will be like his teacher.[192] If we leave out any of the three commands, we are falling short of our commission. Indeed, Jesus warned of the danger of making converts and not disciples: "Woe to you, scribes and Pharisees, hypocrites!

---

[188]Isaiah 33:22 NKJV

[189]Romans 8:28-29 NKJV

[190]Ephesians 4:11-16 NKJV

[191]2 Cor 3:18 NKJV

[192]Luke 6:40 NKJV

For you travel land and sea to win one convert, and when he is won, you make him twice as much a son of hell as yourselves."[193] This is sadly far too common in American Christian churches today.

On the other hand, Christians must still declare the kingship of Christ to their governing officials, even if these same officials have not yet bowed their knees in repentance and faith. As with the Hebrew boys who scolded Nebuchadnezzar (a secular ruler),[194] Christians must speak truth to power and inform their own government of the King of kings. For this proclamation is at least part of the Great Commission: Christ was teaching, "I am the Supreme government official." As the followers of Christ, we are told to go to all nations and instruct people everywhere (yes, even government leaders) *to observe all the things that He has commanded.* This was the message of the early church. It is clear that the modern church has lost sight of these truths.

The corrupt, power mad Jewish leaders killed Christ because he declared himself to be their KING. This was the charge against Him. This is why Pilate asked Him, "Are You the King of the Jews?" To which Christ responded, "It is as you say."[195] Pilate asked the Jews, "Shall I crucify your King?" The chief priests answered, "We have no king but Caesar!"[196] The religious leaders of the day were making the same mistake the religious leaders of today are making. They wrongly believed that human government (Caesar) makes the supreme laws of the land.

Later, secular leaders and officials of Rome, jailed and killed Christ's followers, not for preaching the gospel, but rather because of his LORDSHIP and KINGSHIP. Most secular governments of the first century did not believe in a God who governs the affairs of man. Therefore, they could care less which god or how many gods a person worshipped.[197] Because the early church was proclaiming the lordship and kingship of Christ over all earthy rulers, this is what

---

[193]Matthew 23:15 NKJV

[194]Hebrews 11:34 NKJV

[195]Mark 15:2 NKJV

[196]John 19:15 NKJV

[197]Acts 17:22-23 NKJV

got them in hot water. The power-corrupted government officials of the day did not like the idea that someone was ruling over them from heaven! The early church was turning the world up-side down because they were preaching this message.

> But when they did not find them, they dragged Jason and some brethren to the rulers of the city, crying out, "These who have turned the world upside down have come here too. Jason has harbored them, and these are all acting *contrary to the decrees of Caesar, saying there is another king — Jesus.*[198]

The early church was bold in declaring, "We do not care what Caesar has decreed! Caesar is not the supreme King... Jesus Christ is!" This stance was seen as nothing more than political insurrection. It was for this reason that government officials were throwing the apostles in jail and sentencing them to death—not for the God they worshiped.

History proves that God's laws are binding all over the globe, in all countries, at all times and over all people. When the people of a nation violate these laws, judgment will follow. Justice will be served. No nation is immune from this.

In every place, people understand laws, lawmakers, and the fact that they will be judged by the same. They understand that imprisonment and even death could follow for the most severe offences. Why, then, does it surprise us when we find out the Kingdom of God is any different? I have heard many critics find fault with God for commanding the Israelites to destroy entire nations. Do we understand what these people were guilty of? These were nations full of divine lawbreakers responsible for the most atrocious crimes against humanity. God gave them more than enough time to stop.

God sent Israel to judge the heathen nations because they were sacrificing their children to Moloch.[199] God sent the Babylonians to destroy Israel for the same crimes.[200] God sent the allies to judge

---

[198]Acts 17:6-7 NKJV

[199]Leviticus 18:21 NKJV

[200]2 Chronicles 28:3-4 NKJV

Germany for slaughtering over 10 million Jews and Christians. Why? Because "The judgments of the LORD are true and righteous altogether."[201] When a nation continually lives according to Psalms 2:1-3, God will judge them according to Psalms 2:4-12. God waits for the "cup of iniquity" to become full, and then He sends another nation to execute divine legal justice.

The Christian church in America allowed slavery to continue, and God judged us for it! We got what we deserved. "The judgments of the LORD are true and righteous altogether." Such were the words uttered by Abraham Lincoln in his Second Inaugural Address:

> Both [North and South] read the same Bible and pray to the same God, and each invokes His aid against the other. It may seem strange that any men should dare to ask a just God's assistance in wringing their bread from the sweat of other men's faces, but let us judge not, that we be not judged. The prayers of both could not be answered. That of neither has been answered fully. The Almighty has His own purposes. "Woe unto the world because of offenses; for it must needs be that offenses come, but woe to that man by whom the offense cometh." If we shall suppose that American slavery is one of those offenses which, in the providence of God, must needs come... Fondly do we hope, fervently do we pray, that this mighty scourge of war may speedily pass away. Yet, if God wills that it continues until all the wealth piled by the bondsman's two hundred and fifty years of unrequited toil shall be sunk, and until every drop of blood drawn with the lash shall be paid by another drawn with the sword, as was said three thousand years ago, so still it must be said "the judgments of the Lord are true and righteous altogether.[202]

---

[201]Psalms 19:9 NKJV

[202]Abraham Lincoln, "Second Inaugural Address," (Speech: Washington, DC, March 4, 1865) Teaching American History, http://teachingamericanhistory.org/

Abraham Lincoln understood what few Christian pastors understand today: the message of divine justice. For 250 years, God waited for His people to make things right. Nevertheless, eventually His patience wanes thin. There comes a generation that must pay for the sins of their fathers and for their complacency in not ensuring that justice was served. Jesus taught that "righteous blood shed on the earth, from the blood of righteous Abel to the blood of Zechariah, son of Berechiah, whom you murdered between the temple and the altar," would come upon His generation.[203] Within 40 years, this prophecy came to pass.

During the Civil War, both sides were praying for the war to end. Yet, God allowed it to continue until every dime made off the backs of slaves was squandered on war-strewn fields and every drop of blood spilled by the slave owner's whip was spilled in battle. Ultimately, it was the Christian church (abolitionists) that rose up and judged America, ended slavery, and appeased an angry God.

Do we think that this principle of divine judgment against sinful nations has somehow changed under the New Testament? Have you read the Book of Revelation when the entire world is found guilty?

Fortunately, there will be one place that will be spared from judgment during the end times. It will be like the ark in the days of Noah–a place of sanctuary for God's people. "But the woman [the church] was given two wings of a *great eagle* that she might fly into the wilderness to her place, where she is nourished for a time and times and half a time, from the presence of the serpent."[204] Is this a prophetic reference to America? Not if America refuses to turn and repent before her cup of iniquity is full. If American Christians do not rise up like the abolitionists of old and judge this nation in righteousness, then God will send another nation to do it instead. Justice will be served! At this point, the only thing that will save America is a legal *Appeal to Heaven*.

---

library/document/second-inaugural-address/

[203]Matthew 23:35-36 NKJV

[204]Revelations 12:14 NKJV

The Triune Nature of the Throne of God

The Christian church has also lost the understanding of the triune nature of the throne of God. Many teach that His throne is their local sanctuary or place of worship, and they come before this throne to worship Him. A much fuller picture is provided in scripture, however: God's throne is a seat for a king, as well as for a judge. It is a both a throne room and a courtroom. "His throne was a fiery flame... The court was seated, and the books were opened."[205]

What do we call His seat when He is acting as Judge? In an earthly court setting, we call the judges seat "the bench." In the 1st century, and in the divine courts of heaven, this seat has another name. It is called the judgment seat. A judgment seat is defined as: "A seat or bench in which a judge sits in order to hear arguments and pass down judgment." The term "judgment seat" in the original Greek is not two words, but one. That word is *Bema*, and it means tribunal. A tribunal is defined as: "a seat for a judge in a court." The words *bema* and tribunal connote a courtroom setting in which arguments are heard and judgment is handed down. Our Lord Jesus Christ himself stood before the *bema*, or "judgment seat," of Pilate.[206] The apostle Paul, likewise, stood before the *bema*, or "judgment seat," of both Gallio[207] and Felix[208]. When we die, we will all stand before the Judgment Seat of Christ.[209]

Consequently, there are times when we approach God's throne not as a place of worship but as a courtroom and a place where we go to receive divine justice. The widow of Luke 18 understood this fact. She knew there was an authority higher than herself and higher than her earthly oppressor. She came to this judge in order to plea for a cease and desist letter—a document ordering the cessation of all unlawful activity. In other words, the widow was *appealing* to her ultimate judge. This is how we must understand our *Appeal to Heaven*. We hope to enter the Supreme Court of Heaven and petition the Supreme

---

[205]Daniel 7:9-10 NKJV

[206]John 19:13, Matt 27:19 NKJV

[207]Acts 18:12 NKJV

[208]Acts 25:17 NKJV

[209]2 Cor 5:10 NKJV

Judge for a ruling in our favor. A great resource would be a video series on YouTube videos titled *The Courts of Heaven Session 1-4* by Robert Henderson.

As Christians, we worship a God who is passionate about rescuing the oppressed. He has given us a biblical mandate to approach His throne in order to "seek justice, rescue the oppressed, defend the orphan, and plead for the widow."[210] Seeking justice can only be achieved in a court of law.

Here is where we must expand our understanding of the word *appeal.* The general definition is "an earnest request for aid, assistance, or support."[211] Until now, the Appeal to Heaven movement has been viewed as a prayer movement in which we ask God for aid, assistance, or support. However, the word *appeal,* in the legal system, means taking a case to a superior judge, or court, after receiving an unjust ruling in a lower court.

In the American legal system we have, what is called, an appeals process. If we seek justice in a court of law and do not find it at a lower level, we can ask a higher court to reverse the decision. The highest court in America is the Supreme Court of the United States (SCOTUS). What happens when the highest court in the land makes a series of bad decisions? What happens when our highest government officials are comprised of wicked and unjust men and women? What are we to do when even the SCOTUS outlaws the teaching of the Creator and His laws in our classrooms? What are we do when the SCOTUS legalizes what the divine Lawgiver has called illegal? Abortion exists in America because the church allows it. Pornography exists in America because the church allows it. Are we stuck with these rulings, or is there yet one higher court and one higher judge that we can appeal to?

Throughout history, great men and woman of faith have understood the Appeal to Heaven principle, and have applied it in their own day. Freedom, liberty, and righteousness were the result. The blessings soon followed. Let us now examine, from history, how to apply this principle to our efforts.

---

[210]Isaiah 1:17 NKJV

[211]*Dictionary.com,* "Appeal," http://www.dictionary.com/browse/appeal

The Appeal to Heaven: A Historical View

"In my distress I called upon the LORD, and cried out to my God; He heard my voice from His temple, and my cry came before Him, even to His ears... Nevertheless, He regarded their affliction, When He heard their cry."[212]

— Psalms 18:6; Psalms 106:44

As we have learned in previous chapters, "tyrants" are rulers who refuse to be restrained by divine law and have usurped the sovereignty of heaven. Tyrants either do not understand, have forgotten or refuse to accept the fact that their authority has been divinely delegated; meaning it also has definite limits. In opposition to God's law, tyrants use the power of their office to deny people of their rights; they even persecute believers for obeying God and declaring His truths. The word "tyranny" could, therefore, be defined as "government sanctioned bullying." A thorough study of both biblical and world history will show that heaven does not sanction this type of behavior, nor is God indifferent to it. King David teaches us that the LORD "executes justice for the oppressed, who gives food to the hungry. The LORD gives freedom to the prisoners."[213] Jesus taught that He would avenge

---

[212]Ps 18:6, 106:44 NKJV

[213]Ps 146:7 NKJV

145

(speedily) those who cry out day and night and those hoping to be freed from their oppressors.

The Exodus: A Prototype for Future Deliverance Movements.

Behold, the cry of the children of Israel has come to Me, and I have also seen the oppression with which the Egyptians oppress them.[214]

~ Exodus 3:9

The first recorded account of an Appeal to Heaven movement, in which God delivered His people from tyranny, slavery and bondage, was recorded in the book of Genesis. The story begins when Joseph, the governor of Egypt and second in command to Pharaoh himself, invited his family to Egypt and gave them land during a time of famine and drought. However, after many years,

Joseph died, all his brothers, and all that generation. But the children of Israel were fruitful and increased abundantly, multiplied and grew exceedingly mighty; and the land was filled with them. Now there arose a new king over Egypt, who did not know Joseph. And he said to his people, "Look, the people of the children of Israel are more and mightier than we; come, let us deal shrewdly with them, lest they multiply, and it happen, in the event of war, that they also join our enemies and fight against us, and so go up out of the land." Therefore, they set taskmasters over them to afflict them with their burdens. And they built for Pharaoh supply cities, Pithom and Ramses. But the more they afflicted them, the more they multiplied and grew. And they were in dread of the children of Israel. So the Egyptians made the children of Israel serve with rigor.

---

[214]Ex 3:9 NKJV

> And they made their lives bitter with hard bondage —
> in mortar, in brick, and in all manner of service in the
> field. All their service in which they made them serve
> was with rigor.[215]

Pharaoh had no authority to enslave the children of Israel. The previous administration had invited them to Egypt as guests, and then, contrary to government precedent as well as the explicit laws of God, the current administration enslaved them. In their distress, Israel appealed to heaven, and God heard their voice from His temple and regarded their affliction. At the burning bush, the LORD said the following to Moses:

> And the LORD said: "I have surely seen the oppression
> of My people who are in Egypt, and have heard their
> cry because of their taskmasters, for I know their sor-
> rows. So I have come down to deliver them out of the
> hand of the Egyptians, and to bring them up from that
> land to a good and large land, to a land flowing with
> milk and honey... Now therefore, behold, the cry of
> the children of Israel has come to Me, and I have also
> seen the oppression with which the Egyptians oppress
> them. Come now, therefore, and I will send you to
> Pharaoh that you may bring My people, the children
> of Israel, out of Egypt."[216]

Moses then journeyed back to Egypt to deliver a message from the LORD to Pharaoh: "Thus says the LORD God of Israel: 'Let My people go, that they may hold a feast to Me in the wilderness.'"[217] Pharaoh did not recognize the divine chain of command. He thought he was the highest government official in the land and that he answered to

---

[215]Ex 1:1-14 NKJV

[216]Ex. 3:7-10 NKJV

[217]Ex. 5:1 NKJV

no one. He replied, "'Who is the LORD, that I should obey His voice to let Israel go? I do not know the LORD, nor will I let Israel go.'"[218]

We all know the rest of the story. God judged Egypt with ten plagues until they released the Israelites from captivity. Pharaoh's lawlessness continued on after the plagues. Power mad tyrants with a god-complex do not like it when their "subjects" refuse to comply with their edicts. He sent his army to destroy God's people, but in an act of poetic justice, the trap he set for the children of Israel fell back on his own head. God not only delivered His people from wicked and unjust men, but He also caused the Egyptian army to fall in the pit, submerged by the waters of the Red Sea.

In this story, we see the beginnings of a pattern that will repeat itself repeatedly throughout history:

1. God's people cry out in their oppression.
2. God hears their appeal to heaven.
3. God sends a deliverer to warn the tyrant to cease and desist.
4. The tyrant refuses to cease his, or her, illegal control over God's people.
5. The tyrant uses the power of government (i.e. police, military or the courts) to enforce unlawful edicts.
6. The hand of God is with the deliverer as he leads the people to freedom.

It should not be surprising that the Exodus story has given hope to others throughout human history, especially to Americans. It has encouraged them to use the same Appeal to Heaven principle in order to seek deliverance from oppression, bondage and slavery.

The Pilgrims

As was noted in an earlier chapter, King James I instituted, what he called, the Divine Right of Kings in 1609. This sought to use scripture to demand blind obedience to the crown. However, ever since the invention of the printing press, every Christian had direct access to the

---

[218]Ex. 5:12 NKJV

Bible and no longer had to accept blindly the claims made by a government-backed clergy. Consequently, dissention arose regarding the right of the crown to mandate attendance to Anglican Church services. Many Christian leaders, in an act of civil disobedience, began holding their own religious services. By early 1664, the English Parliament began passing laws such as the *Conventicle Act*, which made it illegal to hold "bible studies" of more than four people.

This dark period in English legal history, in which freedom of religion was greatly curtailed, motivated most of the early American colonists, starting with the first wave of Pilgrims, to flee the tyranny and persecutions of "Christian" Europe. However, they did not advocate overthrowing the king or the English government. The simply wanted to be left alone so they could serve the LORD according to their convictions. They simply said, "Let my people go," and then they fled to the New World. What was their inspiration and motivation? It was the Exodus story. Many of the men who settled colonies in America looked to the example of Israel for inspiration and salvation.

The first recorded example was from Puritan lawyer John Winthrop, in his now famous sermon "A Model for Christian Charity," which he preached as he, and others, fled the tyranny of England. In this sermon, Winthrop expounded the idea that New Testament Christians inherited the divine covenant given to the Hebrews, making them the New Israel.[219] He likened the crossing of the Atlantic to the crossing of the Red Sea. From that moment on, early American colonists would look at their cry for freedom as similar to the cries of the Israelites, prior to their Exodus. In an article titled "How the Exodus Story Created America," by Michael Freund of the Jerusalem Post, we read:

> As Bruce Feiler, the author of America's Prophet: How the Story of Moses Shaped America, has noted, the Pilgrims viewed themselves as reliving the exodus saga. "When they embarked on the Mayflower in 1620," Feiler writes, "they described themselves as the chosen people fleeing their pharaoh, King James. On the Atlantic, their leader, William Bradford, proclaimed

---

[219]Galatians 6:16 NKJV

their journey to be as vital as 'Moses and the Israelites when they went out of Egypt.' And when they arrived in Cape Cod, they thanked God for letting them pass through their fiery Red Sea." Subsequently, when Bradford wrote of Plymouth Plantation, his historical account of the Pilgrims' settling of America, he suggested that there were compelling parallels between the experiences of his own community and that of the ancient Israelites.

A decade later, in 1630, a second wave of Pilgrims made their way across the Atlantic on board the Arbella. While in route to the Massachusetts Bay Colony, John Winthrop delivered a sermon to the passengers entitled "A Model of Christian Charity," in which he too invoked comparisons with the Children of Israel. "We shall find," he said, "that the God of Israel is among us, when 10 of us shall be able to resist a thousand of our enemies, when He shall make us a praise and glory, that men shall say of succeeding plantations: 'The Lord make it like that of New England.'" As if to underline the point, Winthrop concluded his sermon by quoting from "Moses, that faithful servant of the Lord, in his last farewell to Israel."

By all accounts, the Pilgrims were driven by a deep-seated belief that they had a divinely appointed mission. The early settlers were known to refer to Plymouth colony as "Little Israel," and many spoke of Bradford, who became its governor, as "Moses." The Massachusetts Bay Colony, which was located north of Plymouth, was equally imbued with a strong sense of biblical consciousness and identification. As Dr. Gabriel Sivan wrote in his monumental work, The Bible and Civilization, "No Christian community in history identified more with the People of the Book than did the early settlers of the Massachusetts Bay Colony, who believed their own lives to be a literal reenactment of the biblical drama of the Hebrew nation."

The Pilgrims, argues Sivan, saw themselves as "the children of Israel; America was their Promised Land; the Atlantic Ocean their Red Sea; the Kings of England were the Egyptian pharaohs; the American Indians the Canaanites…" Moreover, he suggests, they "saw themselves as instruments of Divine Providence, a people chosen to build their new commonwealth on the Covenant entered into at Mount Sinai." It was this vision and sense of purpose which eventually served as one of the foundations of what came to be known as American Exceptionalism – the belief that the United States is a unique nation blessed by the Creator with a special role to play in the world.[220]

Yet, as we have seen replayed over and over again, power mad tyrants with a god-complex do not like it when their "subjects" seek to be free from their unrighteous administration. The British crown followed God's people to the New World and, from 1620 until the start of the Revolutionary War, used the military and courts to pass restricting laws and impose and administer unlawful edicts.

The American Revolutionary War

In the beginning of the contest with Great Britain, when we were sensible of danger we had daily prayer in this room for the Divine Protection. — Our prayers, Sir, were heard, and they were graciously answered.[221]

— Benjamin Franklin, Constitutional Convention

---

[220]Michael Freund, "How the exodus story created America," *Jerusalem Post,* March 29, 2013, http://www.jpost.com/Opinion/Columnists/How-the-exodus-story-created-America-308136

[221]Benjamin Franklin, "Constitutional Convention Address On Prayer," (Speech: Philadelphia, June 28, 1787) America Rhetoric, http://www.americanrhetoric.com/speeches/benfranklin.htm

More than 150 years after the Pilgrims' arrival at Plymouth, the American colonists realized they could not escape the tyranny of the British crown and parliament. The straw that seemed to "break the camel's back" was *The American Colonies Act*, commonly known as the *Declaratory Act of 1766*. Put simply, the Act proclaimed that Parliament had "full power and authority to make laws and statutes" for the American colonies and was justified in using "sufficient force and validity to bind the colonies and people of America in all cases whatsoever." The colonists thought this abuse of power created conditions akin to slavery.

Thomas Paine articulated the feelings of the American colonists in *The Crisis*, written on December 23, 1776: "Britain, with an army to enforce her tyranny, has declared that she has a right (not only to TAX) but 'to BIND us in ALL CASES WHATSOEVER' and if being bound in that manner, is not slavery, then is there not such a thing as slavery upon earth. Even the expression is impious; for so unlimited a power can belong only to God."[222]

The colonists considered this type of tyranny (government sanctioned bullying) to be the exact opposite of freedom and liberty. When the American colonists refused to comply with such an unlawful infringement of their God-given rights, the tyrant, King James, used his government powers to enforce his unlawful edicts.

According to the Declaration of Independence, King James began "transporting large armies of foreign mercenaries to complete the works of death, desolation and tyranny," and was forcing "fellow citizens," who had been "taken captive on the high seas, to bear arms against their country, [and] to become the executioners of their friends and brethren, or to fall themselves by their hands."[223] The colonists saw this as a criminal act committed by their own government. They reasoned that if an individual were guilty of these acts, they would be called criminals. Why, then, does it become legal when the King's army perpetrates the same?

---

[222]Thomas Paine, *The Crisis* (London: R. Carlisle, 1819), 11.

[223]Thomas Jefferson, *The Declaration of Independence,* Essay, July 4th, 1776, http://teachingamericanhistory.org/library/document/declaration-of-independence/

When the king sent his army to murder, arrest, and burn entire towns, did the America colonists simply accept the situation? Did they believe God required them to accept these criminal acts with passive resignation? The men of Marlborough, Massachusetts unanimously proclaimed in January of 1773, "death is more eligible than slavery. A free-born people are not required by the religion of Jesus Christ to submit to tyranny.... (We) implore the Ruler above the skies, that He would make bare His arm in defense of His Church and people, and let Israel go."[224]

The American colonists did not start an offensive war. They were defending themselves against criminals, who were hiding behind the power of government. Thomas Paine continues, "Not all the treasures of the world, so far as I believe, could have induced me to support an offensive war, for I think it murder; but if a thief breaks into my house, burns and destroys my property, and kills or threatens to kill me, or those that are in it, and to 'bind me in all cases whatsoever' to his absolute will, am I to suffer it? What signifies it to me, whether he who does it is a king or a common man; my countryman or not my countryman; whether it be done by an individual villain, or an army of them?"[225]

Common Sense became the bestselling book in colonial history and galvanized the American colonists against their own government. The American colonists, once again, turned to the story of the Israelites and drew parallels between their circumstances and the story of the Exodus. In his pamphlet/book, Paine described King George III as the "sullen tempered pharaoh of England."[226] This compelled them to write the Declaration of Independence, which essentially told King James, "Let our people go!"

> We, therefore, the Representatives of the United States
> of America, in General Congress, ...declare, That

---

[224]Peter Marshall and David Manuel, *The Light and the Glory*, revised and expanded edition: 1492 – 1793 (Revell, 2009), 324.

[225]Thomas Paine, *The Crisis* (London: R. Carlisle, 1819), 16-17.

[226]Thomas Paine, *The writings of Thomas Paine Vol. I* (London: Putnam's Sons, Knickerbockers Press, 1894), 93.

these United Colonies are, and of Right ought to be Free and Independent States; that they are Absolved from all Allegiance to the British Crown, and that all political connection between them and the State of Great Britain, is and ought to be totally dissolved; and that as Free and Independent States."[227]

Again, what recourse does a Christian people have after all appeals to the earthly government have failed? What can they do when their own leaders sanction tyranny, persecution, and murder? The answer: they can turn to the only proven and effective strategy for deliverance, The Appeal to Heaven!

When they declared their independence from the British government and demanded that King James "let our people go," they warned him that they were calling on God as a judicial arbitrator. They were calling on God to get justice from their adversary. They even enshrined their Appeal to Heaven in the Declaration of Independence: "We, therefore, the Representatives of the United States of America, in General Congress, Assembled, *appealing to the Supreme Judge of the world* for the [righteousness] of our intentions...."[228]

America's founding fathers, recognizing that human governments are not the final authority in the divine chain-of-command, adopted the Appeal to Heaven as a slogan. They realized that years of appeals to the British Government had fallen on deaf ears. The Declaration of Independence made it known to the King of England that they were going over his head. Their appeal, now, would be to King James' boss—the King of kings and Judge of judges! Again, they would reference the Exodus story to justify their course of actions.

On July 4, 1776, shortly after the founders formally adopted the Declaration of Independence, the Continental Congress appointed a committee to create a seal for the newly formed nation. The committee

---

[227] Thomas Jefferson, *The Declaration of Independence,* Essay, July 4, 1776, http://teachingamericanhistory.org/library/document/ declaration-of-independence/.

[228] Thomas Jefferson, *The Declaration of Independence,* Essay, July 4th, 1776, http://teachingamericanhistory.org/library/document/ declaration-of-independence/

consisted of three men: Benjamin Franklin, Thomas Jefferson and John Adams. On August 20, the committee presented the continental Congress their recommendation. Ben Franklin proposed a seal that depicted Moses standing on the shore, extending his hand over the sea, as he was commanded by God, causing the sea to envelop the "Egyptians in the midst of the sea."[229]

Thomas Jefferson submitted a similar theme for his seal. This one would portray the children of Israel in the wilderness, led by a cloud by day and a pillar of fire by night. In his second inaugural address, given on March 4, 1805, he was still equating their national struggle and subsequent victory with that of the Exodus story: "I shall need, too, the favor of that Being in whose hands we are, who led our fathers, as Israel of old, from their native land and planted them in a country flowing with all the necessaries and comforts of life."[230]

The phrase Appeal to Heaven first appeared in the political writings of John Locke. In his published work, *The Two Treatises of Government*, Locke draws from the Bible to illustrate the principle:

> What is my Remedy against a Robber, that so broke into my House? Appeal to the Law for Justice. But perhaps Justice is denied, or I am crippled and cannot stir, robbed and have not the means to do it. If God has taken away all means of seeking remedy, there is nothing left but patience. But my Son, when able, may seek the Relief of the Law, which I am denied: He or his Son may renew his Appeal, till he recovers his Right. But the Conquered, or their Children, have no Court, no Arbitrator on Earth to appeal to. Then they may Appeal… to Heaven, and repeat their Appeal, till they have recovered the native Right of their Ancestors.[231]

---

[229]Ex 14:26-29 NKJV

[230]Thomas Jefferson, "Second Inaugural Address," (Speech: Washington, DC, March 4, 1805) http://avalon.law.yale.edu/19th_century/jefinau2.asp

[231]John Locke, "Two Treatises of Government" in *The Works of John Locke. A New Edition, In Ten Volumes. Vol. V.* (London: 1823), 183.

Great leaders have long since understood the importance of symbolism. Flags are a very powerful way to represent ideas. Consider the wholesale attempt to remove the Confederate flag (sic) from America. For some, it is not about removing a flag, as much as an attempt to remove the ideas, thoughts, images, and memories that the flag conveys. Adolph Hitler also understood the powerful concept of symbolism. This is why he flew the Nazi swastika flag over all of Germany.

The power of symbolism was not ignored by the Founding Fathers. While many Americans today will recognize the "Don't Tread on Me" flag, some of the earlier flags, which represent God's active involvement in the outcome of the war, have been obscured from history. The Bedford Flag is the oldest known flag in the United States. The Bedford Minuteman Company flew it. The flag depicts the arm of God reaching out of the clouds, holding a sword. The original is housed at the Bedford, Massachusetts Town Library. America's second oldest flag in American history is the Appeal to Heaven Flag. This flag depicts an evergreen tree, or pine tree, with the motto *Appeal to Heaven* or sometimes, *An Appeal to God*, displayed on it. A brief explanation the importance of the pine tree may be needed here.

In an attempted to retain her world dominance, England needed a powerful navy. The tall, straight, and very strong pine tree was perfect for the making of ships' masts. Due to lack of suitable lumber on the British Isles, the English crown instituted a law, called the "Mast Preservation Clause", in the Massachusetts Charter in 1691. It reserved all trees over 24 inches as the "King's property", even though they existed on private land. Clearly, the King believed he had the right to take whatever he wanted from whomever he wanted. This is much like the story of Robin Hood, where hunting or cutting down trees in the "King's woods" was illegal, and the "sheriff" would be sent to fine or arrest anyone taking the King's property. Government surveyors would patrol the "King's Woods" and place the symbol of a broad arrow on larger trees, designating them as the property of the Crown. This essentially became another form of taxation.

Prior to harvesting trees for their own needs and livelihoods, law required the colonists, to seek permission to cut down any trees on their property. Once the King's Surveyor came out and marked the larger trees, the colonists were still required to purchase a royal license to harvest those. For the colonists, to use modern lingo, this law created an enormous amount of "red tape". They even had to wait for permission before harvesting firewood to heat their own homes.

In general, legalists do not care about people; they care about controlling people. To them, "the rules are the rules," and they are more concerned about others obeying the rules than their overall health or safety. It is better for a family to freeze to death than violate the King's edicts! This is the defining difference between laws and legalism. Laws are created for the benefit of the people; legalism is the response of government officials to laws, their grasping attempt to control their subjects. Jesus, in contrast, cared more about people than he did about man-made or "legalistic" rules. This was the source of many of his confrontations with the government officials of his day, who could see no justifiable reason to violate the law — who would even have advised David and his men to starve to death.[232]

For this reason, individual citizens must determine which laws are just, for the benefit of society, or unjust. In one of the first of many acts of civil disobedience, the colonists disregarded the "Mast Preservation Clause" and practiced what they called "Swamp Law". They harvested pines on their property, even those with the King's mark, without obtaining a license. Unsurprisingly, the colonists paid for this decision by paying steep fines. As could be expected, the tyrant used his government forces, the sheriffs, to enforce his unlawful edicts.

The fines only motivated further acts of civil disobedience. In New Hampshire, this led to what is called the Pine Tree Riot of 1772, remembered as one of the first acts of organized civil disobedience against British policy. It occurred two years before the Boston Tea Party and three years before "the shot heard around the world."

The *Appeal to Heaven* principle so captivated the minds of the founders, that in October, 1775, with memories of the Pine Tree Riots still very fresh, George Washington, the acting commander-in-chief of the Continental Army, commissioned six of his warships to display

---

[232]Matt 12:1-14 NKJV

the *Appeal to Heaven* Flag during their conflict with the British. To the Christian colonists, this was no mere religious rhetoric. Rather, it was a genuine prayer movement. From that time, until the end of the war, our founding fathers met daily for prayer. Benjamin Franklin, himself, testified to this fact while addressing the Constitutional Convention in 1787: "In the beginning of the contest with Great Britain, when we were sensible of danger, we had daily prayer in this room for our divine protection. Our prayers, Sir, were heard, and they were graciously answered."[233]

How did a nation of "farmers with pitchforks" defeat the greatest military superpower of the day? Our founding fathers cited two reasons. First, their cause was righteous. Second, they firmly believed that applying the *Appeal to Heaven* principle resulted in God moving on behalf of the newly created American nation.

Today's secularists would have us to believe that God does not exist and that He does not intervene in the affairs of men. Benjamin Franklin disagreed. He continued, "All of us who were engaged in the struggle must have observed frequent instances of a superintending Providence in our favor."[234] In other words, Franklin believed that all who were engaged in the Revolutionary War must have observed frequent instances when their *Appeal to Heaven* had been successful. Was he the only founder with this testimony?

America's first Supreme Court Justice, John Jay, commented, "This glorious revolution... distinguished by so many marks of the Divine favor and interposition... and I may say miraculous, that when future ages shall read its history they will be tempted to consider a great part of it as fabulous."[235] He further stated that God had intervened in the conflict, and then he drew a parallel to the Exodus story: "The many remarkable... events by which our wants have been supplied and our enemies repelled... are such strong and

---

[233]Benjamin Franklin, "Constitutional Convention Address On Prayer," (Speech: Philadelphia, June 28, 1787) America Rhetoric, http://www.americanrhetoric. com/speeches/benfranklin.htm

[234]Benjamin Franklin, "Constitutional Convention Address On Prayer," (Speech: Philadelphia, June 28, 1787) America Rhetoric, http://www.americanrhetoric. com/speeches/benfranklin.htm

[235]Walter Stahr, *John Jay: Founding Father,* (New York: Diversion Books, 2012)

striking proofs of the *interposition of Heaven*, that our having been hitherto delivered from the threatened bondage of Britain ought, like the emancipation of the Jews from Egyptian servitude, to be forever ascribed to its true cause."[236]

On August 1, 1776, Samuel Adams stated the following in a speech at the State House in Philadelphia:

> There are instances of, I would say, an almost astonishing providence in our favor; our success has staggered our enemies, and almost given faith to infidels; so we may truly say it is not our own arm which has saved us. *The hand of Heaven* appears to have led us on to be, perhaps, humble instruments and means in the great providential dispensation which is completing. We have fled from the political Sodom; let us not look back lest we perish and become a monument of infamy and derision to the world.[237]

George Washington was so convinced that God had intervened in the war that he considered "infidels" all those who refused to admit as much: "The Hand of providence has been so conspicuous in all this, that he must be worse than an infidel that lacks faith, and more than wicked, that has not gratitude enough to acknowledge his obligations."[238]

In the American story, we can once again see the *Appeal to Heaven* principle utilized by people held in captivity:

1. God's people cry out in their oppression
2. God hears their *Appeal to Heaven*

---

[236]Edwin Wiley, *The United States,* Vol 2, (New York: American Educational Alliance, 1909) 62

[237]Samuel Adams, "Speech about the Declaration of Independence," (Speech: Philadelphia, August 1, 1776) Samuel Adams Heritage Society, ://www.samuel-adams-heritage.com/documents/speech-about-declaration-of-independence.html

[238]Richard Vetterli and Gary Bryner, *Search of the Republic, Public Virtue and the Roots of American Government,* (Rowman & Littlefield Publishers, 1987), 68.

3. God sends a deliverer to warn the tyrant to cease and desist.
4. The tyrant refuses to cease his illegal institutional control over God's people.
5. The tyrant uses his government office to enforce his unlawful edicts.
6. The hand of God is with the deliverer as he leads the people to freedom.

America's founding fathers were so deeply influenced by the Exodus story, following the example of a people who likewise faced oppression thousands of years. Neither would the significance of the Exodus story be lost on the next generation of oppressed people—the American slaves and the good men and women who sought to deliver them from their oppression.

The American Civil War

"Seek justice, Rebuke the oppressor; Defend the fatherless, Plead for the widow."[239]

Isaiah 1:17

Using an article titled by Bruce Feiler, we now transition from the Revolutionary war to the Civil War era:

Moses was an American icon long before there was an America. When the Pilgrims left England in 1620, they described themselves as the chosen people fleeing their pharaoh, King James. On the Atlantic, they proclaimed their journey to be as vital as "Moses and the Israelites when they went out of Egypt." Moreover, when they got to Cape Cod, they thanked God for letting them pass through their fiery Red Sea. By the time of the Revolution, Moses had become the go-to narrative of American freedom. In 1751, the

---

[239]Isaiah 1:17 NKJV

Pennsylvania Assembly chose a quote from the Five Books of Moses for its State House bell, 'Proclaim Liberty thro' all the Land to all the Inhabitants Thereof – Lev 25:10.'

The future Liberty Bell was hanging above the room where the Continental Congress passed the Declaration of Independence on July 4, 1776. Congress' last order of business that day was to form a committee of Thomas Jefferson, Benjamin Franklin and John Adams to design a seal for the new United States. The committee submitted its recommendation that August: Moses, leading the Israelites across the Red Sea. In their eyes, Moses was America's true Founding Father... a reluctant George Washington led the colonists to victory and then presided over the drafting of the Constitution. The parallel was not lost. Two-thirds of the eulogies at Washington's death compared him to Moses.

Although Moses was a unifying presence during the founding era, a generation later, he got dragged into the issue that most divided the country. The Israelites' escape from slavery was the dominant motif of slave spirituals, including "Turn Back Pharaoh's Army," "I Am Bound for the Promised Land" and the most famous, "Go Down, Moses," which was called the national anthem of slaves…, Yet as abolitionists used the exodus to attack slavery; Southerners used it to defend the institution. The War Between the States became the War Between the Moses. It took America's most Bible-quoting president to reunite the country. Abraham Lincoln talked about the exodus at Gettysburg, and, when he died, he too was compared to Moses.[240]

---

[240]Bruce Feller, "Moses is America's prophet," *CNN,* March 29, 2010, http://www.cnn.com/2010/OPINION/03/29/feiler.moses.easter.passover/

In the 1857 case of Dred Scott v. Sanford, the Supreme Court decided in a 7-2 decision that African Americans were not persons, and therefore had neither rights nor any legal protection under the Law. As the nation prepared for war, the Exodus story in antebellum America was repeatedly used by both slaves and slave-owners, each drawing from the biblical story to justify their cause.

During the Civil War, it was reported that Abraham Lincoln answered a question, posed by members of the Connecticut Temperance Union, on whether he thought God was on the side of the North or the South. He responded, "Sir, my concern is not whether God is on our side. My greatest concern is to be on God's side, for God is always right."[241] Lincoln understood that it is incumbent upon man to discern God's will in every situation and then align himself accordingly.

While later skeptics have questioned the validity of this quote, Scripture is very clear that this is indeed an immutable truth. God takes sides. The apostle Paul, for instance, taught us, "What then shall we say to these things? If God is for us, who can be against us."[242] This also applies in times of war. Much earlier, King David spoke of God's deliverance in battle, acknowledging the partisan character of divine intervention.[243] This eternal truth is predicated on man acting in step with the LORD's eternal purposes. The great mistake of the South was listening to their Christian pastors, who were far more concerned with appeasing their rich slave owning elders, deacons, and congregation members, than they were in seeking and appeasing Almighty God.[244]

---

[241]Abraham Lincoln Presidential Library Foundation, 2016, http://www.alplm. org/272viewessay.aspx?id=800

[242]Romans 8:31 NKJV

[243]Psalms 124 NKJV

[244]As evidence for this claim, please see *The Key to Uncle Tom's Cabin* by Harriet Beecher Stowe. This was the non-fictional follow-up book to *Uncle Tom's Cabin*, written in response to the slave owners, who claimed all the characters in her book had no basis in reality. Stowe includes firsthand quotes from resolutions passed by a number of southern denominations concerning slavery.

The slaves saw Abraham Lincoln as Moses, themselves as the Israelites, and the slave owners as Pharaoh, the hard taskmaster. However, the confederates saw the anti-slavery North as Egypt and Abraham Lincoln as Pharaoh.[245] Like the founding fathers before them, they declared independence from the United States and thought God would be on their side. They were *appealing to heaven* for the righteousness of their intentions. Unfortunately, their intensions were anything but righteous. They were violating divine law.

As we discussed previously, there were two types of slavery in the Old Testament: indentured or voluntary servitude, and forced servitude, or slavery. Under Mosaic Law, kidnapping a person, or even owning a kidnapped person, was punishable by death.[246] In the New Testament, this was called kidnapping, or man-stealing, depending on your choice of translation: "But we know that the law is good if one uses it lawfully, knowing this: that the law is not made for a righteous person, but for the lawless and insubordinate, for the ungodly and for sinners, for the unholy and profane, for murderers of fathers and murderers of mothers, for manslayers, for fornicators, for sodomites, *for kidnappers*, for liars, for perjurers, and if there is any other thing that is contrary to sound doctrine, according to the glorious gospel of the blessed God which was committed to my trust."[247]

Yet, the truth of God was suppressed by "untaught and unstable people," who twist words and intentions "to their own destruction, as they do also the rest of the Scriptures."[248] The southern plantation owners would "heap to themselves teachers, having itching ears," and would "turn their ears away from the truth, and be turned aside to fables."[249] Reverend R. Furman is one example of the many Ministers

---

[245]John Coffey, *Exodus and Liberation: Deliverance Politics from John Calvin to Martin Luther* (Oxford: Oxford University Press, 2014), 139-142.

[246]Exodus 21:16 NKJV

[247]1 Timothy 1:8-11 NKJV

[248]2 Peter 3:16 NKJV

[249]2 Timothy 4:3-4 NKJV

who preached, "The right of holding slaves is clearly established in the Holy Scriptures, both by precept and example."[250]

This deception from the pulpit induced an entire populace to defend, to the death, an institution that God had outlawed. Confederate President Jefferson Davis said the following in his Inaugural Address: "(Slavery) was established by decree of Almighty God…. It is sanctioned in the Bible, in both Testaments, from Genesis to Revelation…. It has existed in all ages, has been found among the people of the highest civilization, and in nations of the highest proficiency in the arts."[251]

In his "*Meditation on the Divine Will*," written in September of 1862, Abraham Lincoln wrote, "The will of God prevails. In great contests each party claims to act in accordance with the will of God. Both may be, and one must be, wrong. God cannot be for and against the same thing at the same time."[252] It was clear the God could not be for and against slavery. One side was tragically wrong.

As it was with slave-owners, so it was with the slaves. They oftentimes used the Exodus story to justify their desire for freedom from tyranny. The Exodus story not only became a source of hope, but also provided them with the blueprint that would ultimately lead to their deliverance- the Appeal to Heaven.

The demise of slavery began when Christian abolitionist preachers from the North, both white and black, began to travel through the southern states. These Black evangelists violated southern laws (civil disobedience) when they began preaching the Gospel to slaves in secret late-night meetings.

Although it was illegal for slaves to read the Scriptures for themselves, they attended church services on the plantation where only "slavery friendly" bible verses were used, such as Ephesians 6:5:

---

[250]Richard Furman, "The Views of the Baptists, Relative to the Coloured Population in the United States in a Communication to the Governor of South Carolina," Furman University, http://history.furman.edu/~benson/docs/rcd-fmn1.htm

[251]Jefferson Davis, "Inaugural Address," (Speech: Montgomery, February 18, 1861) Avalon Project, http://avalon.law.yale.edu/19th_century/csa_csainau.asp

[252]"Meditation on the Divine Will," Abraham Lincoln Online, 2016, http://www.abrahamlincolnonline.org/lincoln/speeches/meditat.htm

"Slaves, obey your earthly masters with respect and fear, and with sincerity of heart, just as you would obey Christ."[253] However, at the late-night meetings, the abolitionist preachers told them that they were made in the image of God and were created equal to the white man.

One of the favorite stories used by these northern preachers was the story of the Exodus. The African slaves identified fully with the plight of the Israelites. The story ignited hope within their souls. Had not the children of Israel been enslaved by pharaoh? When they appealed to heaven, did God not send a deliverer to lead them out of captivity and into the Promised Land? Why would God not do the same for them? As their faith grew, so did their belief that the God of Abraham, Isaac, and Jacob was now their God too.

These Christian slaves would oftentimes gather to cry out to God for freedom. "Again I say to you that if two of you agree on earth concerning anything that they ask, it will be done for them by My Father in heaven. For where two or three are gathered together in My name, I am there in the midst of them."[254] While this activity was clearly a violation of southern laws—the participating slaves knew they could face the whip, or worse, —they continued to meet and humbly worship God.

The early prayers of these slaves, or their Appeal to Heaven, often took the form of song Spirituals, such as *Turn Back Pharaoh's Army*, *I Am Bound for the Promised Land,* and *Go Down, Moses*. These songs gave them an identity, which linked them to a historical past. In time, they also would be free—in large part by the work of the abolitionists.

Abolitionists

The abolition of slavery began with the Quakers At first, they viewed slavery as a matter of individual conscience, but then began to see the abolition of slavery as their Christian duty to God. It was their duty to "seek justice" and rebuke the "oppressors."

---

[253]Eph 6:5 NKJV

[254]Matthew 18:19-20 NKJV

The abolitionist movement in America began in earnest during the 1820s and 30s, and was dominated by Bible-believing Christians, who were moved to "seek justice and rebuke the oppressor."[255] They advocated obedience to God over obedience to man. They understood from Romans 13 that God was the highest authority in the universe, and that human governments, including the federal congress or the SCOTUS, did not have the authority to legalize what God has called illegal. They advocated civil disobedience as a means to end slavery. They defied federal law by starting the Underground Railroad. For these reasons, they were persecuted. Here is how PBS aptly described the early abolitionists:

> Radicals. Agitators. Troublemakers. Liberators. Called by many names, the abolitionists tore the nation apart in order to make a more perfect union. Men and women, black and white, Northerners and Southerners, poor and wealthy, these passionate antislavery activists fought body and soul in the most important civil rights crusade in American history. What began as a pacifist movement fueled by persuasion and prayer became a fiery and furious struggle that forever changed the nation.... In the face of personal risks — beatings, imprisonment, even death — abolitionists held fast to their cause, laying the civil rights groundwork for the future and raising weighty constitutional and moral questions that are with us still.[256]

One such Abolitionist was a woman, named Harriet Tubman. An escaped slave herself, she dedicated her life to leading as many slaves as possible to freedom via the Underground Railroad. On June 1, 1863, Tubman, along with Union Colonel James Montgomery and 300 black Union soldiers, led a raid to free 720 slaves. This raid freed 10 times more slaves then her previous 10 years working on the

---

[255]Isaiah 1:16-17 NKJV

[256]"The Abolitionists," PBS, http://www.pbs.org/wgbh/americanexperience/features/introduction/abolitionists-introduction/

Railroad. She would later say that as she watched the former slaves—men, women and children—streaming to freedom from the country-side, it reminded her of the children of Israel streaming out of Egypt.

Josiah Wedgwood

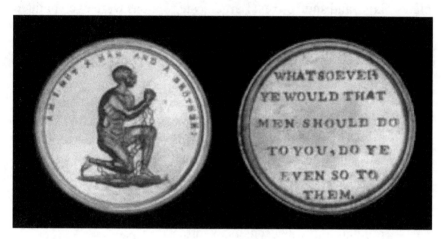

Another influential British abolitionist, a man named Josiah Wedgwood, not only made an appeal to heaven, but also made an appeal to his fellow man. Wedgwood was a prominent friend of Thomas Clarkson, a leading abolitionist campaigner who, with the help of William Wilberforce, played a decisive role in ending slavery in England. Wedgwood is perhaps best remembered for creating and circulating an anti-slavery medallion. The medallion depicts a shackled slave kneeling on his knees with the inscription "Am I Not a Man and a Brother?" On its reverse side, the medallion was embossed with the inscription, "Whatsoever ye would that men should do to you, do ye even so to them." This Christian message of human equality was drawn from several of Christ's teachings found in Luke 6:31 and from Matthew 12:7, which reads: "So in everything, do to others what you would have them do to you, for this sums up the Law and the Prophets."[257]

The purpose of the medallion was to tug at the heartstrings of other Christians and force them to reconsider the morality of

---

[257]Matt 12:7 NKJV

enslaving their brothers and sisters in Christ. Wedgewood understood the importance that symbolism plays in promoting an idea or a cause. The medallion was designed not only to spread the abolitionist message, but also to encourage people to share their ideals. Indeed, the image began popping up everywhere. It was printed on plates, flags, and snuffboxes. Large-scale replicas were even painted on walls, the equivalent of the modern billboard. As a piece of jewelry, too, the medallion became a real fashion statement, as Thomas Clarkson noted:

> Ladies wore them in bracelets, and others had them fitted up in an ornamental manner as pins for their hair. At length the taste for wearing them became general, and thus fashion, which usually confines itself to worthless things, was seen for once in the honorable office of promoting the cause of justice, humanity and freedom. The design on the medallion became popular and was used elsewhere.[258]

Ever since, civil rights activists have understood the importance of symbolism and have used it to advance their cause. They also have accepted the inevitability of immediate setbacks and failures, recognizing that civil movements rarely succeed all at once. Rather, these movements usually progress through three major stages.

First, the movement is mostly ignored and disregarded, and the initial enthusiasm of its most ardent backers will fade away and come to nothing. "And now I say to you, keep away from these men and let them alone; for if this plan or this work is of men, it will come to nothing; but if it is of God, you cannot overthrow it — lest you even be found to fight against God."[259]

Second, when outsiders realize the movement is gaining grassroots support and when they can ignore it no further, they will oppose and vilify it. "Blessed are those who are persecuted for righteousness'

---

[258]David Dabydeen, "The Black Figure in 18th Century Art," BBC, 2011, http://www.bbc.co.uk/history/british/abolition/africans_in_art_gallery_02.shtml

[259]Acts 5:38-39 NKJV

sake, for theirs is the kingdom of heaven. Blessed are you when they revile and persecute you, and say all kinds of evil against you falsely for My sake. Rejoice and be exceedingly glad, for great is your reward in heaven, for so they persecuted the prophets who were before you."[260]

If the cause is just and its advocates persevere to the end, it will finally be met with success. "This charge I commit to you, son Timothy, according to the prophecies previously made concerning you, that by them you may wage the good warfare, having faith and a good conscience.... Fight the good fight of faith, lay hold on eternal life, to which you were also called and have confessed the good confession in the presence of many witnesses."[261]

All great movements that have been successful in abolishing tyranny have had two common features: they appealed both to *God* and to *man*. The American fathers were successful because they not only appealed to God, but they also appealed to their fellow citizens through writings like *Common Sense*. They worked hard to establish a grassroots movement to promote the cause of freedom. Likewise, the abolitionists were successful because they not only appealed to God, but also to their fellow men and women through writings like *Uncle Tom's Cabin*.

History has a funny way of repeating itself. Today's government officials and media, guided more by political correctness than justice, are either too corrupt or too cowardly to fulfill their sworn duties. As we respond to these problems, we must follow the examples of our predecessors and appeal both to God and to man. To achieve the latter, we must not neglect the appropriate use of symbolism.

Martin Luther King

In the late 1950s, both black and white Christians began to feel, like their 19th century counterparts, a call to "seek justice" and "rebuke the oppressor" from the residue effects of the Civil War— the second-class citizenship of African Americans. This time, the

---

[260]Matthew 5:10-12 NKJV

[261]1 Timothy 1:18-19; 6:12-13 NKJV

oppression came in the form of harsh segregationist laws in the American South. It was the Christian church that spearheaded a grass-roots movement to support the cause of freedom—a call to action against government officialdom, the proprietors of which were either too corrupt or too cowardly to fulfill their moral, legal, and constitutional duties.

It should come as no surprise that black clergy, and laity alike, drew inspiration from the story of the Exodus, the only historically proven model for achieving victory over tyranny. They once again sought a Moses who could lead them into the social, economic and political "Promised Land."

In January of 1957, Dr. Martin Luther King, Jr. invited 60 black ministers and other Christian leaders to the Ebenezer Church in Atlanta to discuss racial injustice. One month later, a civil rights organization called the Southern Christian Leadership Conference was born. From a second meeting emerged a liberator in the person of MLK himself, the first president of the nascent organization. He was well suited to the task, for he understood from history "that freedom is never voluntarily given by the oppressor; it must be demanded by the oppressed."[262]

MLK contended not only with the secular forces of government, but also with an ignorant and apathetic clergy. On January 16, 1963, a group of white ministers published *The White Ministers' Law and Order Statement*, in which they condemned MLK's actions. This statement contained many glaring falsehoods that Dr. King would be address personally two months later in his, now famous, *Letter from a Birmingham Jail*.

Perhaps the most glaring falsehood rebutted by MLK was the notion that government is the highest authority in the land, and that Christians may not defy government officials who have broken and ignored God's laws.

MLK also articulated a profound understanding of his high calling. On the night before his assassination, he compared himself to the Hebrew prophet:

---

[262]Martin Luther King Jr. *Letter From a Birmingham Jail*, April 16, 1963, African Studies Center, https://www.africa.upenn.edu/Articles_Gen/Letter_Birmingham.html

Like anybody, I would like to live a long life. Longevity has its place. However, I'm not concerned about that now. I just want to do God's will. And He's allowed me to go up to the mountain. And I've looked over. And I've seen the Promised Land. I may not get there with you. But I want you to know tonight, that we, as a people, will get to the Promised Land! And so I'm happy, tonight. I'm not worried about anything. I'm not fearing any man! Mine eyes have seen the glory of the coming of the Lord![263]

Soviet Communism

Many historians credit the demise of the communism to the political efforts of the West. However, those living in East Germany knew the real reason that this tyrannical form of government failed: *An Appeal to Heaven.* I will allow the participants to tell their own story in an article titled "PRAYER: The Power Behind a Peaceful Revolution" by Marshall Foster of the World History Institute.

This year marks the 25th anniversary of the fall of the Berlin Wall. Many see that dramatic event as the most symbolic victory for liberty in the 20th century. The peaceful dismantling of the wall was followed by the complete disintegration of the Soviet Union, resulting in the liberation of tens of millions of people and the birth of freedom in many Eastern European nations. Through those miraculous events the world was saved from the terrifying threat of thermonuclear holocaust.

Many historians credit the demise of the Berlin Wall to a devastated Soviet economy, coupled with President Ronald Reagan's call for Mr. Gorbachev to "tear down that wall!" However, there is a virtually

---

[263]Martin Luther King Jr. *I've Been to the Mountaintop,* (Speech: Memphis, April 3, 1968) AFSCME, http://www.afscme.org/union/history/mlk/ive-been-to-the-mountaintop-by-dr-martin-luther-king-jr

unknown story behind East Germany's liberation in 1989. I first learned of it several years ago when I was in Germany preparing for a Reformation Tour I was about to lead. In Leipzig, Germany, I visited a beautiful 16th century Lutheran cathedral and heard a lecture by the pastor, Rev. Christian Fuhrer. After the lecture, Pastor Fuhrer and I met privately and he told me about a remarkable prayer movement that began with a handful of people in his church in 1982, seven years before the wall came down.

For almost 40 years the tyrannical, Soviet- dominated German Democratic Republic (GDR) had ruled East Germany with an iron fist. Under Dictator Erick Honecker, death or imprisonment awaited anyone who dared to defy the GDR or attempt to cross the wall between East and West Germany. Rev. Fuehr decided to begin a simple prayer meeting called Prayers for Peace. Every Monday at 5 p.m. the faithful would gather, light 40 candles representing the Jews' 40 years in the wilderness, and pray for peace.

For some time, the meetings were largely ignored by East German authorities; but eventually attendance at the weekly prayer meeting grew to thousands and the GDR could not turn a blind eye. Government spies infiltrated the meetings and recorded names of those present. Agents of the GDR tried to intimidate Pastor Fuhrer, once leaving him out in the snow to die. Numerous adults who attended the meetings were fired from their jobs, even though there was no political agenda, only prayers for freedom. Soon, German youth took the place of their parents because they had no jobs to lose. Despite persecution and seemingly no answer from God, the intercession continued for seven years and the meetings turned into a prayer movement.

On October 9, 1989, Pastor Fuhrer convened the weekly prayer meeting. This time, however, he handed out candles to each attendee. He instructed each person to light their candle as they left the gathering and to join other East Germans in the streets of Leipzig. Together they would peacefully march to the city center.

As the 2,000 prayer warriors emerged from Pastor Fuhrer's church, they were met by approximately 100,000 fellow candle-carrying Germans. Facing possible death, the peaceful army approached the GDR troops. Never had Honecker allowed this kind of defiance. Previously, troops would have shot demonstrators against the regime. Russian tanks were lined up behind the soldiers who pointed their machine guns at the ever-growing crowd. The demonstrators bravely approached the soldiers (their fellow Germans) and offered them lighted candles. Amazingly, one by one, soldiers began to put down their weapons and receive the lighted candles. Soon all the soldiers had lowered their weapons and joined with the protestors. The Russian tanks backed up and returned to their barracks. Fuhrer said that East German officials would later say that they were ready for anything, "except candles and prayer."

The next week Honecker resigned, knowing that he had lost the loyalty of the German army. He knew that he could no longer intimidate anyone, least of all people armed with the power of prayer! A month later, Soviet Premier Gorbachev began tearing down the Berlin Wall, and the German people knew that the miraculous, courageous events of October 9, 1989, had been the true power leading to Germany's reunification.

Without the church it would have been like all other revolutions before – bloody and unsuccessful. "We did it," Fuhrer said, "because the church has to do it." Now, 25 years after the miracle at Leipzig, Fuhrer warns the church of lethargy:

"Today that feeling of belonging together has largely given way to a shallow materialistic prosperity. Faith in the future and in the power and possibilities that God can bestow on us has disappeared. But the church is only the church if it is there for other people... The church must be open to all and must champion the disadvantaged. When an individual has no other aims, visions or hopes than those relating to his next holiday, shopping spree or share prices he will begin to cease to exist. That is why we need the vision of Jesus: a vision not only of sharing but of taking on responsibility for each other so that faith and hope...can sweep through the masses again like a fresh wind."

Enslaved for 70 years under the Nazis and Communists, the East German people were ultimately blessed by a faithful praying remnant and guided by God's gracious hand. Their country was restored and our world was transformed, and it began with the power of prayer. In light of this history, cannot believing Americans peacefully pray and courageously act to restore our liberty under God? May God help us to do just that for His glory and for our children's children.[264]

---

[264]Marshal Foster, "Prayer: The Power Behind a Peaceful Revolution," http://storage.cloversites.com/worldhistoryinstitute/documents/WHI_03Mar014_Journal_4.pdf.

The Appeal to Heaven Prayer

Vindicate us Lord, and plead our cause against an ungodly nation. Get justice for us from our adversaries. Deliver us from deceitful and unjust men. Cause them to fall into the pit that they have dug for the righteous. Grant to Your servants that we may speak Your word with all boldness. Give us the nations for our inheritance, and the ends of the earth for our possession.

In the year 2000, Bruce Wilkinson wrote a small book titled *The Prayer of Jabez*. What followed was simply amazing. His work reenergized the Christian church in her understanding of the power of prayer—how even one man is able to move heaven on his behalf. Believers from all around the world began praying the exact same prayer to Almighty God. I firmly believe that God is stirring up another such unified prayer movement. However, this prayer will not be offered on behalf of an individual, but rather on behalf of a nation, and maybe on behalf of all nations. Jesus Christ talked about the power of unified prayers in Matthew:

> Most assuredly I tell you, whatever things you will bind on earth will be bound in heaven, and whatever things you will release on earth will be released in heaven. Again, assuredly I tell you, that if two of you will agree on earth concerning anything that they will

ask, it will be done for them by my Father who is in heaven. For where two or three are gathered together in my name, there I am in the midst of them.[265]

Can you imagine the power that would come upon our nation, and the world, should God's people ever come together in a spirit of unity, everyone uttering the same *biblically inspired prayer* for our nation and the world? Where would we get such a prayer?

The story of how the Appeal to Heaven prayer came to be, started many years ago when I began to pray fervently for the future of America. It seemed to me then, and still does now, that all of our government leaders were either consciously or subconsciously moving America further and further away from the Lord. This departure from His precepts would ultimately result in America's judgment, much like Sodom and Gomorrah before us.

On October 4, 1997, I joined over three million Christian men as we descended upon Washington, DC for, what was called, "Stand in the Gap: A Sacred Assembly of Men." Just as Abraham stood outside of Sodom, interceding for that wicked city, millions of Christian men interceded on that day, asking our Heavenly Father to be merciful upon political Sodom (Washington, DC) as His people of faith seek to restore our nation under the Lordship of Christ.

The central scripture verse for the rally came from 2 Chronicles, which is God's recipe for national restoration. It reads: "If My people who are called by My name will humble themselves, and pray and seek My face, and turn from their wicked ways, then I will hear from heaven, and will forgive their sin and heal their land."[266]

In recent years, many of America's political and religious leaders have joined me in sounding the alarm that our nation is in extreme peril, in danger of impending destruction and judgment. Several years ago, our church showed the Isaiah 9:10 Judgment movie produced by World News Daily's Joseph Farah, edited and directed by award-winning filmmaker George Escobar, and

---

[265]Matthew 18:18-20 NKJV

[266]2 Chronicles 7:14 NKJV

featuring messianic Rabbi Jonathan Cahn, author of the New York Times bestseller "The Harbinger: The Ancient Mystery That Holds the Secret of America's Future." This movie eventually became the most popular faith movie of 2012. Its central message was a sober one. It was an indictment on America, a warning that like ancient Israel before us, we would receive God's judgment unless we repent of our wicked ways. The director's solution for the American crisis likewise drew from 2 Chronicles 7:14, God's recipe for national healing and restoration.

As I watched this movie, I received further confirmation of what I had said in my 2006 book. It also heightened my conviction that America was in more trouble than I previously suspected. I fervently increased my intercession for this nation, and I asked God what He would have us do. However, I oftentimes found myself at a loss for words. I found myself saying, "LORD, your word tells us *to* pray, but it does not tell us *what* to pray. I do not know what I should be asking for." In effect, I was making the mistake of telling God what He should do rather than asking, "Lord, what do You want me to do?"[267]

From my years of biblical education, I understood that God would oftentimes tell us what to pray in certain situations. In order to grasp this fact, it is of vital importance that we first understand the difference between the *verb* prayer and the *noun* prayer.

The *verb* prayer is an action. It is something that we do. The *noun* prayer is not something that we do; rather, it is something that we have. More specifically, it is something we receive. How can one receive a prayer? When Jesus' disciples asked him to teach them to pray, they were not asking Him how to go through the motions of prayer, they were asking Him what words were to be used when petitioning the Father.[268] They knew *how* to pray, but they did not know *what* to pray. What Jesus gave them was a very specific prayer. "Our Father in heaven, Hallowed be Your name, Your kingdom come, Your will be done, on earth as it is in

---

[267]Acts 9:6 NKJV

[268]Luke 11:1 NKJV

heaven...." They (and we) should be taking these words before the throne of Heaven.

In our Peacemakers Outreach *Faith Training* seminars, I teach that when God gives us very specific words to pray, it is, what James calls, the Prayer (noun) of Faith.[269] The Prayer of Faith is not something that we do; it is something that we receive. When we pray for the sick, for example, we should not come before the heavenly throne and tell God what we would have Him do. Instead, we are to ask God what He would have us do. In every situation (including health issues), God knows what the problem is and He knows the solution. The Prayer of Faith is God identifying the problem and giving us the proper words to say. Jesus did not use the same formula to heal everyone. He first had to diagnose the root cause of the problem, before he was able to administer a cure.

Understanding this principle, I began to tell God: "You know what America's problem is and how to fix it. Help me to pinpoint the root cause of America's fall, so that I will have a better understanding of how to pray for the nation." At first I was expecting to be given specific words to say; until, that is, I realized that scripture is full of divinely inspired prayers that can be used for any number of situations, such as the *Prayer of Jabez*. One question remained: "What is America's problem, and what are we instructed to pray in these situations?"

Not all prayers are created equal; some are good, some are bad, and some others are appropriate, or not, depending on the nature of the request. God knows the root of all problems and can direct us to the specific prayer that best fits the circumstances. He knows exactly who the enemies are, where they are hiding, and from where they are attacking. Therefore, the solution is to *ask God what to pray* (the words to use).

Many years ago, I began compiling notes for an upcoming book entitled *The Prayers of God*. It is based upon the presupposition that *All Scripture is given by inspiration of God*.[270] This being true, then every one of the prayers listed in the Holy Scriptures

---

[269]James 5:15 NKJV

[270]2 Timothy 3:16

are divinely inspired and are profitable for dealing with specific problems. As people of faith, we have a book full of these prayers. The Psalms especially are a compilation of worship songs and prayers that were divinely inspired and uttered by King David when faced with very specific situations. Since only God knows what the root cause of every problem is, He also knows what prayers we should use. We just need to find, through the guidance and direction of the Holy Spirit, what prayers fit our particular situation, circumstance, or need. I have not heard a better real-life illustration of how to apply this principle, than that given by the late, great saint Brian Bailey.

Bailey told of a government official with a god-complex. This official wrongfully assumed he was the highest authority on earth and he began to handle his affairs accordingly, ignoring and disobeying the directives of his superiors. He was denying Bailey the right to enter the country lawfully. Ultimately, Brother Bailey would be vindicated by means of a divinely inspired prayer, as he described in his own words:

> Many years ago I had the privilege of ministering in a certain country. Because I was a foreigner, I needed a visa to remain there. However, the local government official refused my application, which lawfully had every right to be accepted, because he did not like English people. The senior pastor told me that if I had given the official some money all would have been well. But I could not do [bribe him] because I am a Christian. Fortunately, there was a member in our congregation who knew the Justice Minister of the country very well. He provided me with an introduction, and with it I was ushered into the Chief Secretary's office. After I explained my request, he said that I was lawfully entitled to that visa. Then he wrote a note to that official with orders to grant my request. But the local official replied that he was not concerned with what the government officials in the capital said, he

was the lord in the city where I was the assistant pastor and he would not issue the visa. Therefore, I could no longer remain in that country. At that time, I was offered a position in an organization in another country. The Lord indicated that I should accept it, so I left for that nation. Many months later I had an occasion to pass through the frontier of the previous country. The Custom's Official, seeing my passport, told me that I could not enter the country again since my name had been posted at every frontier of that nation. Naturally I was very confused and when I prayed that night, the Lord led me to pray verse one of Psalm 43. *"Vindicate me, O God, and plead my cause against an ungodly nation; oh, deliver me from the deceitful and unjust man!"* (referring to the corrupt government official who was refusing to follow the law.)

Some weeks later I received a letter from that first official who had originally refused my visa, saying that I could come to his office at my convenience and receive my visa. This I did, and I took the occasion to ask him what had caused his change of heart. He replied that when he had posted my name on every frontier he was obliged to notify the British Counsel General. This official in turn was stirred up by God to protest to the local Governor that this official had done this to a pastor. The Governor, in turn, had his spirit stirred up by God to order the local official to grant my request for a visa. *Thus we see the power of a Spirit-directed prayer, which can even change the minds of government. Beloved, under the direction of the Spirit we should pray scriptural prayers, and we will see God work mightily on your behalf!"*[271]

---

[271]Brian J. Bailey, *Psalms: Book One chapter 1-50*, 1996, 323-325

In the Scripture, we should be able to find prayer that is capable not only of pinpointing the root of America's problem, but also of changing the minds of those government officials who have been deceived into thinking they are the highest authority in all matters. While many of America's religious leaders have been praying, and continue to pray, for our nation, our prayers seem to be having no effect. Today, America is far closer to resembling ancient Sodom and Gomorrah than the "city on a hill" that was envision by the Pilgrims or by our Founding Fathers. Despite years of prayers for America, we are still on the verge of impending collapse and judgment. Why? Is it because God no longer hears our prayers, or is it because our prayers are not specific enough? Scripture is clear that it is possible to ask and not receive, because we ask amiss[272]. In other words, we are not asking for the right thing, or we are asking with impure motives. Up to this point, what righteous God-fearing Americans have lacked is a specific, unified, and divinely inspired prayer for our government leaders.

As believers, we are commanded in scripture to pray for our government leaders and for those in positions of authority: "Therefore I exhort first of all that supplications, prayers, intercessions, and giving of thanks be made for all men, for kings and all who are in authority, that we may lead a quiet and peaceable life in all godliness and reverence."[273]

Again, what are we to pray for? It depends upon the situation. Are our leaders abiding under the divine chain-of-command and the authority of heaven? Are they wicked and unjust leaders who seek to displace the rightful heir from His throne? If the latter were true, then our prayers for these leaders should necessarily reflect that reality.

My question for the LORD was how to pray for the present leaders of the US government. The Spirit of God then led me to Psalm 2:1-3, which not only pinpoints the problem, but also instructs believers what they are to pray for in such circumstances. King David prophesied of a future time of worldwide rebellion by

---

[272]James 4:3 NKJV

[273]1 Timothy 2:1-4 NKJV

the world's political leaders: "Why do the nations rage and the people plot a vain thing? The *kings of the earth* set themselves, and *the rulers* take [legal] counsel together, Against the LORD and against His Anointed, saying, 'Let us break their bonds in pieces and cast away their cords from us.'"[274]

This passage recounts the vain attempt of the world's leaders to replace God and act as a law unto themselves, typified today by attempts to remove the Ten Commandments from courthouses and Nativity scenes from city squares. Consider attempts to eliminate prayer and the bible from our schools or eliminate 'under God' from the Pledge of Allegiance. There has been a wholesale rebellion by our world leaders, who have sought to nullify the laws of God and force believers into compliance with their lawlessness. Their actions represent nothing less than a political insurrection against the laws of God.

As I was working on this manuscript, I received an email newsletter titled "The Great Revolt" from our friends at Francis Frangipane Ministries. The newsletter clearly describes the world's condition upon Christ's return and provides a powerful insight regarding what the church should pray for in these last days. The following is adapted from Francis Frangipane's book, *The Days of His Presence*:

> As though Jesus were reading a news summary of recent years, His prophecies of two thousand years ago clearly describe our times. Thus, we are compelled to discern accurately the significant era in which we live. Indeed, of the many prophetic fulfillments of our day, one in particular rises with undimmed candor. I am speaking of what the Bible calls the "apostasy." Recall Paul's warning: "*Let no one in any way deceive you, for [the day of the Lord] will not come unless the apostasy comes first*" (2 Thess. 2:3). The apostasy has traditionally been described as a time of deception and massive falling

---

[274]Psalms 2:1-3 NKJV

away from authentic faith in Christ. Depending upon your specific view, sometime before or after the apostasy the rapture of the church will occur.

However, the concept of apostasy as merely "a falling away" is incomplete. The original Greek word for apostasy, *apostasia*, when used in classical Greek literature, meant "a political revolt." From this we understand that the end-time apostasy is not just a time of sinfulness or large scale backsliding; it is actually a time of open defiance and warlike aggression against godliness in general. In other words, the *apostasia* is a political insurrection against the laws of God.

This interpretation of the apostasy is not an isolated view. The New International Version, Revised Standard Version, Phillips Translation, and New English Bible all render *apostasia* as "the rebellion." The Living Bible interprets the apostasy as the "great rebellion," while the Jerusalem Bible assigns a proper name to this era: "The Great Revolt." As we consider the fulfillment of so many other prophecies, let us carefully observe: mankind has entered an era of open revolt and outright rebellion — an apostasy — against the moral standards of God.

Today, we are witnessing a large-scale rebellion against traditional moral values. Indeed, this brazen attitude has had a name for itself since the 1960s: the sexual revolution. Moreover, "revolution" is exactly what it is. Our moral standards have not only been challenged, they have been replaced by a nonstandard. Indeed, the *great rebellion* seeks to legitimize and then mainstream every perversity known to man!

The Second Psalm, perhaps more than any other Bible text, accurately portrays the spirit of our time. Indeed, it also proclaims our correct response to Satan's bold advance. Although it was quoted by the early church (Acts 4:25-26), God has set its full realization for the end of this age. "Why are the nations in an uproar and the peoples devising a vain thing? The kings of the earth take their stand and the rulers take counsel together against the Lord and against His Anointed, saying, 'Let us tear their fetters apart and cast away their cords from us!'" (Ps. 2:1-3).

Although "the rebellion" reveals itself worldwide in many ways, in America many of our leaders have certainly been counseling together "against the Lord" in their decisions... This railing against God has not gone unnoticed in Heaven. Is the Almighty confounded? Has fear concerning recent developments gripped the Lord's heart? No. The Psalm continues: "He who sits in the heavens laughs, the Lord scoffs at them. Then He will speak to them in His anger and terrify them in His fury" (Ps. 2:4-5).

The Lord laughs at the foolishness of those in full revolt, as they imagine God's judgments cannot reach them. Why then, you ask, does the Lord delay His full judgment? In part, the Lord waits for us, His church. For while the world shall demand, and receive, the reign of hell, the goal of the praying church shall be for the reign of Heaven. You see, all prophecies shall be fulfilled: not only those concerning evil but also those concerning righteousness. The Lord has purposed to have a "bride without spot or wrinkle" and a "kingdom" of wheat without tares.[275]

---

[275]Francis Frangipane, *The Days of His Presence*, (Charisma House, 2012) 55-56

Presently, America, along with the rest of the major world governments, has fallen into the age old cycle in which rebellion, in the form of humanism and paganism, threatens to bring divine judgment upon the nations of the world. In Chapter 3, we discussed at length the divine chain-of-command set forth in Romans chapter 13. Recall Illustration #1, which pictures the proper and lawful chain-of-command when all parties are submitting to God and His divine order.

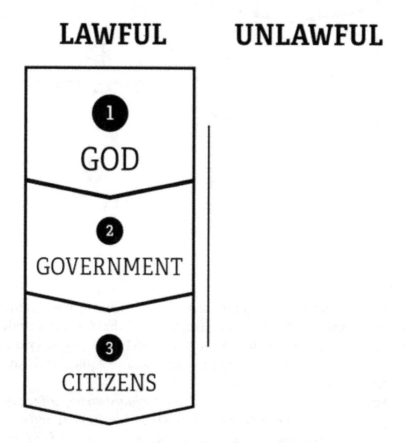

At the other end of the spectrum, Illustration #4 showed an entire world in rebellion against the laws of God.

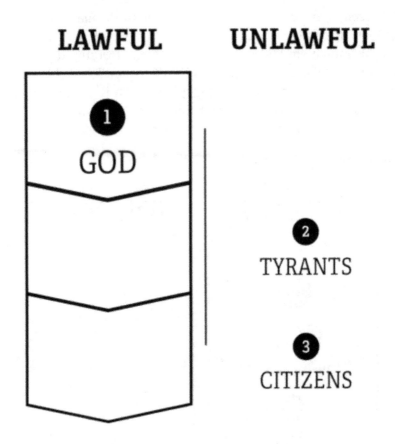

LAWFUL **UNLAWFUL**

GOD

TYRANTS

CITIZENS

If this is our present day political situation, what recourse is there for the saints? With a firm understanding of the *divinely inspired prayer* principle, I began to seek the LORD for a prayer (words) that would be needed to restore our nation. The Appeal to Heaven Prayer was born.

Vindicate us Lord, and plead our cause against an ungodly nation. Get justice for us from our adversaries. Deliver us from deceitful and unjust men. Cause them to fall into the pit that they have dug for the righteous. Grant to Your servants that we may speak Your word with all boldness. Give us the nations for our inheritance, and the ends of the earth for our possession.

Every word and phrase in this prayer come from the Holy Scriptures, and was used when God's people found themselves in the very same situation that the people of faith in America find themselves in today. The *Appeal to Heaven* prayer can be categorized into three sections:

1. Prayer for the nation
2. Prayer for government leaders
3. Prayer for ourselves

With this in mind, let us dissect the *Appeal to Heaven* prayer line by line.

"Vindicate us Lord, and plead our cause against an ungodly nation.... Deliver us from deceitful and unjust men. – The first two parts of our *Appeal to Heaven* prayer come from Psalm 43:1: "Vindicate me, O God, and plead my cause against an ungodly nation: O deliver me from the deceitful and unjust man." This prayer is thought to have been prayed by David, as the jealous and vindictive government official (King Saul) sought to kill him without just cause. In this portion of the prayer, we are asking God to deliver His people from deceitful and unjust men who seek to persecute them without just cause.

Through his prayer, David took his case before the supreme judge and arbitrator. To be "vindicated" means to be cleared, absolved, or exonerated of all specious charges. David had done nothing wrong and was asking God to both vindicate and deliver him from an unjust and wicked government leader. King Saul sought to kill David for the same reason that the government leaders sought to kill Christ – envy.[276]

Neither David nor Christ were guilty of any crime against their persecutors. Yet, they needed to be vindicated from the false accusations of these *deceitful and unjust man*. As we have seen, Christians in America are becoming increasingly more vilified by *deceitful and unjust* persons in our government and court system simply for the

---

[276]Matthew 27:18, 1 Samuel 18:1-11, Luke 19:37-40 NKJV

biblical, social, moral, and cultural positions they are taking. We are being persecuted and prosecuted for no just reason.

Like every saint before us, we can likewise expect to be vilified for our defense of the word of God and for the testimony which we hold. Scripture teaches that this will get much worse as we enter the last days, even to the point of persecution and martyrdom by corrupt officials and judges, who themselves hate Christ and refuse to live under His authority. Jesus routinely warned us that this would be the case *before* the end would come:

> If the world hates you, you know that it hated Me before it hated you.... But this happened that the word might be fulfilled which is written in their law, "They hated Me without a [just] cause."[277]

> You will be brought before *rulers and kings* for My sake, for a testimony to them. And the gospel must first be preached to all the nations. But when they arrest you and deliver you up, do not worry before-hand, or premeditate what you will speak. But what-ever is given you in that hour, speak that; for it is not you who speak, but the Holy Spirit. Now brother will betray brother to death, and a father his child; and children will rise up against parents and cause them to be put to death. And you will be hated by all for My name's sake. But he who endures to the end shall be saved.[278]

> Then they will deliver you up to tribulation and kill you, and you will be hated by all nations for My name's sake. And then many will be offended, will betray one another, and will hate one another. Then many false prophets will rise up and deceive many. And because lawlessness will abound, the love of

---

[277]John 15:18, 25

[278]Mark 13:9-13 NKJV

many will grow cold. But he who endures to the end shall be saved. And this gospel of the kingdom will be preached in all the world as a witness to all the nations, *and then the end will come.*[279]

"Vindicate us Lord, and plead our cause against an ungodly nation – The word *nation* is a reference to government leaders and not to individual citizens. The first question that has to be asked, therefore, is whether those who control the reins of the American government are godly or ungodly. Are our government leaders legislating under their proper-delegated authority, or are they ruling and reigning like the leaders in Psalms 2:1-3? Consider the chart below as we compare current political topics in light of God's precepts:

GODLY   UNGODLY

GODLY	UNGODLY
Belief / Acknowledgment of God (1 Peter 1:21)	Atheism / Rejection of God (Psalms 14:1, 78:22)
Creation Taught in Schools (Genesis 1:1, 25)	Evolution Taught in Schools (Romans 1:25)
God's View of Marriage / Man and Woman (Matthew 19:5)	Homosexual Marriage (Leviticus 18:22; Romans 1:26-27)
Anti-Abortion (Deuteronomy 30:19)	Pro-Abortion (Exodus 1:16; Matthew 2:16)
Moral Absolutes (Ecclesiastes 12:13)	Situational Ethics (Proverbs 12:15)
Freedom / Liberty (John 8:36)	Slavery / Bondage / Tyranny (Galatians 5:1)
Government under Divine Guidance (Proverbs 14:34)	Separation of Church and State (Micah 4:12)
Jesus Christ as Lord (Psalms 144:15)	Man as God (Genesis 3:5)
Nation under God (Psalms 33:12)	Nation without God (Isaiah 1:4; Psalms 9:17)
Blessed by God (Deuteronomy 28:1-14)	Cursed by God (Deuteronomy 28:15-67)

[279]Matthew 24:9-14 NKJV

From the time of the first settlers, until the years leading up to World War II, America was clearly in the left hand column at every level of government. After the SCOTUS coup d'état, in which this rebel branch declared itself the unchallengeable rulers of America, our country has systematically and progressively moved out from under divine authority. The SCOTUS is pro-evolution, pro-abortion, pro-pornography, pro-homosexuality, pro-humanism, anti-family, anti-God, and anti-religion. *These are not the traits of a godly nation or godly leaders.* "When the righteous are in authority, the people rejoice; But when a wicked man rules, the people groan."[280] Hence our prayer for God to deliver us from these deceitful and unjust men.

Deliver us from deceitful and unjust man – All of mankind finds themselves in one of two categories: the just and the unjust.[281] When Christ returns there will only be two groups—the wheat and the tares, the sheep and the goats, the just and the unjust, the righteous and the unrighteous. It is clear that the lines between good and evil are becoming increasingly apparent as Americans, and even the Christian church, is polarizing on morality issues. Today, each and every American is choosing a side. Which camp will you be found in?

There are those who *daily* pray for God's will to be *done on earth as it is in heaven*, and those who actively and deliberately seek to oppose the Kingdom of God and His precepts. All of those who oppose God find themselves in one of two categories: the deceived and the deceivers. Oftentimes it is difficult to tell the difference between the two. The deceived are operating in ignorance and do not even know they are being deceived. *They have yet to see the light.*

Consider a Pharisee named Saul who persecuted the church and even killed many of the saints simply for spreading the gospel of Christ.[282] Yet, after his Damascus Road conversion, he became the Christian church's first theologian and the divinely inspired author of over half of the New Testament.

---

[280]Proverbs 29:2 NKJV

[281]See Matthew 5:45 & Acts 24:15 NKJV

[282]Acts 8:1-3 & Galatians 1:13 NKJV

On the other hand, there are the deceivers. The deceivers will not embrace the truth even after it is clearly presented to them, and they try their utmost to induce others to follow their sinful path. Jesus warned that this deception would be one of the key signs of the end of the church age. *"For false christs and false prophets will rise and show signs and wonders to deceive, if possible, even the elect."*[283] Just like Lucifer, these men will use scriptures to cajole people away from the true faith. Regrettably, many of these individuals are Christian ministers who are guilty of deceiving entire congregations and denominations.[284] Both Paul and Jude warned of these men.[285]

On an individual level, when we pray for God to *deliver us from deceitful and unjust men,* we are asking God to protect us from deception. An extension of this prayer would be: "Lord, please do not allow me to be deceived by these *deceitful and unjust* people." In America today, there are many people in high placed and reputable institutions — our churches and education system, the media and government — who seem to say all of the right things because they know what people want to hear. They are men and women who employ biblical and constitutional language simply to control the masses. They have taken their playbook from professed communists who realized, in Eastern Europe after World War II, that it is important to control both sides of the argument. Otherwise, those who truly oppose tyranny will rise up with real solutions instead of mere rhetoric.

On a national level, this portion of the prayer is a cry for God to reveal who is who. Who is trying to restore our Constitutional Republic and who is using the constitution and the scriptures to control and subjugate the American people lest real, solution based opposition arise? These *wolves in sheep's clothing* are our true adversaries. Because of their intentional and deliberate deception of the people, they will receive a much greater judgment.

"Get justice for us from our adversaries." – As the children of God, we can expect to have human adversaries on this earth. They are

---

[283]Mark 13:22 NKJV

[284]1 Timothy 6:10, 12; 2 Timothy 2:18 NKJV

[285]Acts 20:29-31, 2 Corinthians 11:13-15 & Jude 3-13 NKJV

called *the children of the devil*. It truly bothers me when I hear religious leaders say that "We are all God's children." I am not sure where they are getting their information. Jesus told the religious leaders of His day, "You are of your father the devil, and the desires of your father you want to do. He was a murderer from the beginning, and does not stand in the truth, because there is no truth in him. When he speaks a lie, he speaks from his own resources, for he is a liar and the father of it."[286] It is clear that "we are all not God's children."

These two bloodline have been at odds with one another since Cain and Able. The children of the devil have always sought to kill the children of God, never the other way around.[287] The creation eagerly waits for the revealing of the sons of God.[288] Who will they be? Here is a hint, *They will be Peacemakers*.[289]

Appealing to Heaven in prayer and asking Him to get justice from these *deceitful and unjust* adversaries is an act of faith. It is what Jesus commanded us to do when we are oppressed.

When the Son of Man comes, will He really find faith on the earth? Do we really believe God will deliver us from our adversaries? Some Christians think it a pious act to sit idly by and let others abuse you. The widow who came to the judge and asked for justice from her adversary did not simply take matters in her own hand, but neither did she sit idly by and allow a wicked man to oppress her. She appealed for justice. She called for an arbitrator. She Appealed to Heaven!

True, we are not to avenge ourselves when we are wronged, but God, on the other hand, is more than free to avenge us. "Repay no one evil for evil. Have regard for good things in the sight of all men. If it is possible, as much as depends on you, live peaceably with all men. Beloved, do not avenge yourselves, but rather give place to wrath; for it is written, 'Vengeance is Mine, I will repay,' says the Lord."[290] Many of God's saints throughout biblical history understood, and applied, both portions of this truth to their individual lives.

---

[286]John 8:44-45 NKJV

[287]1 John 3:10-12 NKJV

[288]Romans 8:19 NKJV

[289]Matthew 5:9 NKJV

[290]Romans 12:17-20 NKJV

David–When Saul sought to kill David, he did not repay *evil for evil*, but rather called the LORD to act as arbitrator and judge between them:

Let the LORD judge between you and me, and let the LORD avenge me on you. But my hand shall not be against you. As the proverb of the ancients says, 'Wickedness proceeds from the wicked.' But my hand shall not be against you. After whom has the king of Israel come out? Whom do you pursue? A dead dog? A flea? Therefore, let the LORD be judge, and judge between you and me, and see and plead my case, and deliver me out of your hand.[291]

Paul – The apostle did not seek vengeance upon Alexander the coppersmith, but allowed for the LORD to repay him for his wickedness. *"Alexander the coppersmith did me much harm. May the Lord repay him according to his works."*[292] Paul understood *it is a righteous thing with God to repay with tribulation those who trouble His sons and daughters.*[293]

We must never forget God's prerogative to weigh out justice and vengeance. "He who leads into captivity shall go into captivity; he who kills with the sword must be killed with the sword. Here is the patience and the faith of the saints."[294] It will be "poetic justice" when God's true children are avenged because the wicked, by their actions, have determined their own judgment.

"Cause them to fall into the pit that they have dug for the righteous." – Some will attempt to counter this portion of the "Appeal to Heaven" prayer with Romans 12:17-21. We must make a clear distinction between us taking vengeance and God taking vengeance. Romans 12, 1 Peter 3:9, and Matt 5:43-48, along with many other scriptures, tell us how to respond personally to our enemies. It is the hope that our love for our enemies will so overcome them, that we will win them to our side. However, if they continue to do evil for our good, then God

---

[291]1 Samuel 24:12-15 NKJV

[292]2 Timothy 4:14 NKJV

[293]2 Thessalonians 1:6 NKJV

[294]Revelation 13:10 NKJV

will avenge us. "Whoever rewards evil for good, Evil will not depart from his house." (Prov 17:13)

As Christians, we are not to take vengeance into our own hands. This is God's domain. This scripture teaches that we are not to avenge ourselves. It does not say, however, that it is wrong to be avenged or vindicated from wicked government leaders who have attacked us for unjust cause. When the fifth seal is opened in the Book of Revelation, those who had been slain for the word of God and for their testimony cried with a loud voice, saying, "How long, O Lord, holy and true, until You judge and avenge our blood on those who dwell on the earth?"[295]

The principle of "poetic justice" can be found in many literary works, including the Bible. It happens when, in an ironic twist of fate, a villain's punishment mirrors his or her own conduct towards an adversary. This principle was taught by our LORD in Matthew 7:1-2. "Judge not, that you be not judged. For with what judgment you judge, you will be judged; *and with the measure you use, it will be measured back to you.*" Therefore, we must be very careful when we measure out judgment lest the same measure be used against us.

Our prayer for our adversaries **"to fall into the pit that they have dug for the righteous"** is simply asking God to turn their own wicked plans against them. This principle was taught in Psalm 35:7-8: *"For without* [just] *cause, they have hidden their net for me in a pit, which they have dug without* [just] *cause for my life. Let destruction come upon him unexpectedly, and let his net that he has hidden catch himself; into that very destruction let him fall."* Again, this is the principle of reaping what we sow. *"Do not be deceived, God is not mocked; for whatever a man sows, that he will also reap."*[296] It is God who will cause the unrighteous to fall into the pit that they have dug for the righteous.

God is a God of Poetic justice. He will see to it that both *individuals* and *nations* will receive rewards and punishments for their conduct to their fellow man.[297]

---

[295]Revelation 6:9-10 NKJV

[296]Galatians 6:7 NKJV

[297]Matthew 25:31-46 NKJV

Nations – "The nations have sunk down in the pit which they made; in the net which they hid, their own foot is caught. The LORD is known by the judgment He executes; the wicked is snared in the work of his own hands."[298]

Individuals – "Behold, the wicked brings forth iniquity; Yes, he conceives trouble and brings forth falsehood. He made a pit and dug it out, and has fallen into the ditch that he made. His trouble shall return upon his own head, and his violent dealing shall come down on his own crown."[299]

Scripture is full of examples where wicked and unjust men have plotted against the saints without just cause, only to find that in an ironic twist of fate, their own devious plans have been turned against them. The measures they used to judge others were turned against them. Here are two examples.

Daniel – Because Daniel had proven himself more capable than all other government officials, King Darius placed him over his whole realm. Daniel's peers, being envious of his righteousness and his promotion, plotted and conspired against him without just cause. They tricked king Darius to pass a law making prayer illegal. Anyone found guilty of breaking this law would be cast into the lion's den.[300] Daniel, knowing that his right to pray comes from the Creator and that no earthly authority had the authority to forbid it, committed an act of civil disobedience. Daniel appealed to heaven, and in an ironic twist of fate, God caused the wicked, along with their wives and children, to fall into the very same ditch that they had dug for Daniel—or in this case, they fell into the lion's den.[301]

Mordecai and Esther – Haman was a government official with a god-complex. He wanted everyone below him, from a lower station, to bow and pay homage to him. Mordecai refused. Haman not only

---

[298]Psalms 9:15-16 NKJV

[299]Psalms 7:14-16 NKJV

[300]Daniel 6:1-9 NKJV

[301]Daniel 6:23-24 NKJV

sought to kill Mordecai, but all of God's people without just cause.[302] Haman's equally wicked wife Zeresh suggested that gallows be made to hang Mordecai.[303] In response, God's people appealed to heaven and fasted for three days. Esther then appealed to king Ahasuerus to *get justice for me from me adversaries*.[304] In an ironic twist of fate, God caused the wicked Haman, along with his ten sons, to fall into the ditch he laid for the righteous—or in this case, the gallows, which he had built for the righteous Mordecai.

> Look! The gallows, fifty cubits high, which Haman made for Mordecai, who spoke good on the king's behalf, is standing at the house of Haman." Then the king said, "Hang him on it!" So they hanged Haman on the gallows that he had prepared for Mordecai.... The wicked plot which Haman had devised against the Jews should return on his own head, and that he and his sons should be hanged on the gallows.[305]

These two stories serve as a grim warning against government officials who seek to persecute and kill the righteous without just cause. In both cases, God's righteous judgment was not only measured out on the guilty parties, but also on their families.

Send out Your light and Your truth–God's word is portrayed as both light and truth. We are recipients of the oracles of God, and as believer we have been mandated to carry the messages of the gospel of repentance to a dark and dying world. Unfortunately, many do not want to hear the truth and will make themselves enemies of God and His people. The apostle Paul notably asked, "Have I therefore become your enemy because I tell you the truth?"[306] In America today, the wicked boldly flaunt their sin while the Christian is accused of hate,

---

[302]Esther 3:1-6 NKJV

[303]Esther 5:12-14 NKJV

[304]Esther 7:6 NKJV

[305]Esther 7:9-10, Esther 9:13-14, 25 NKJV

[306]Galatians 4:16 NKJV

simply for speaking the truth. For this reason, many churches and pastors have lost their salt, and hide their light under a basket for fear of being called names.

Grant to Your servants that we may speak Your word with all boldness.–We have forgotten that we have been given the authority to speak boldly in the Lord's name, exhorting people to live righteous, holy lives and to rebuke those who do not: "Speak these things, exhort, and rebuke with all authority. Let no one despise you."[307] This type of boldness is not natural. It is a divine boldness that is given to us when we are filled with the Holy Spirit. Otherwise, the disciples would not have needed to ask for it. Unfortunately, the courage and boldness that was exhibited by the early church has turned into fear and cowardice.

Give us the nations for our inheritance, and the ends of the earth for our possession – Psalm 2 not only predicts the rebellious condition of the world's leaders, but also gives the saints their instruction as to what their response should be:

"Why do the nations rage, and the people plot a vain thing? The kings of the earth set themselves, and the rulers take counsel together, Against the LORD and against His Anointed, saying, "Let us break their bonds in pieces and cast away their cords from us." He who sits in the heavens shall laugh; The LORD shall hold them in derision. Then He shall speak to them in His wrath, and distress them in His deep displeasure: "Yet I have set My King on My holy hill of Zion." "I will declare the decree: The LORD has said to Me, 'You are My Son, Today I have begotten You. Ask of Me, and I will give You the nations for Your inheritance, and the ends of the earth for Your possession."[308]

The command that we have been given is clear. We are to ask the nations for our inheritance and the ends of the earth for our possession! James tells us that *we have not because we ask not.*[309] Jesus

---

[307] Titus 2:15 NKJV

[308] Psalms 2:1-8 NKJV

[309] James 4:3 NKJV

instructs us, "*Ask, and it will be given to you; seek, and you will find; knock, and it will be opened to you.*"[310] All of the verbs (ask, seek, knock) are written in the present imperative tense, which denotes continued action. "Ask and keep on asking, seek and keep on seeking, knock and keep on knocking." This is the *effective, fervent prayer* spoken of by James and modeled by Elijah.[311]

We are told to Appeal to Heaven to be given the nations for our inheritance and the ends of the earth for our possession. We have to understand that part of our inheritance is to rule and reign with Christ over the nations.[312] Those who rule will understand and apply the Romans 13 Doctrine of Higher Authority to their individual lives.

The time of the early church virtually mirrors the political atmosphere in the world today, a time when government leaders considered themselves to be gods and religious authorities used His name to control the masses. Psalm 2:1-3 was as much a reality in the apostle's day as it is in ours. No portion of scripture better summarizes everything that we have taught up to this point:

So [the government leaders] called them and commanded them not to speak at all nor teach in the name of Jesus. However, Peter and John answered and said to them, *"Whether it is right in the sight of God to listen to you more than to God, you judge. For we cannot but speak the things which we have seen and heard"* [civil disobedience]. So when they had further threatened them, they let them go, finding no way of punishing them, because of the people, since they all glorified God for what had been done. For the man was over forty years old on whom this miracle of healing had been performed. Being let go, they went to their own companions and reported all that the chief priests and elders had said to them. So when they heard that, they raised their voice to God with one accord [Appealed to Heaven in unity] and said: "Lord, You are God, who made heaven and earth and the sea, and all that is in them, who by the mouth of Your servant David have said: *'Why did the nations rage, and the people plot vain things? The kings of the earth took their stand, And the rulers*

---

[310]Matthew 7:7 NKJV

[311]James 5:13, 1 Kings 18:41-46 NKJV

[312]Matthew 5:5, 2 Timothy 2:12, Revelation 20:4-6 NKJV

were gathered together Against the LORD and against His Christ.' "For truly against Your Holy Servant Jesus, whom You anointed, both Herod and Pontius Pilate, with the Gentiles and the people of Israel, were gathered together to do whatever Your hand and Your purpose determined before to be done. Now, Lord, look on their threats, and grant to Your servants that with all boldness they may speak Your word, by stretching out Your hand to heal, and that signs and wonders may be done through the name of Your Holy Servant Jesus." And when they had prayed, the place where they were assembled together was shaken; and they were all filled with the Holy Spirit, and they spoke the word of God with boldness.[313]

When we study the actions and responses of the early church, when government officials sought to deprive them of the freedom of religion and their freedom of speech, we see that their actions were three-fold:

1. They clearly understood and applied the Doctrine of Higher Authority to their cause: "Whether it is right in the sight of God to listen to you more than to God, you judge."
2. They defied and ignored immoral and illegal laws: "For we cannot but speak the things which we have seen and heard."
3. They called God as an arbitrator by raising their voice to God with one accord: "Now, Lord, look on their threats, and grant to Your servants that with all boldness they may speak Your word."[314]

As we have proved through the whole of human history, every great Christian leader has understood that only by applying this three-fold Appeal to Heaven principle, has an enslaved people ever been freed from their wicked and unjust oppressors.

---

[313]Acts 4:18-31 NKJV

[314]Acts 4:29 NKJV

United in Prayer, United in Hope

"There has never been a spiritual awakening in any country or locality that did not begin in concerted, sustained and united prayer"[315]

~ A.T Pearson

As I woke this morning and turned on my television, I was reminded that today is the 31st anniversary of Martin Luther King's "I have a dream" speech. This speech (along with my study of his Letter from the Birmingham Jail) reinforced my conviction that one person, with the faith and the courage to confront unjust civil authorities by using biblical truth like a sword, can change the future of a nation for the better. We believe that it is time that many like-minded people arise once again in order to return America to greatness.

Samuel Adams is quoted as saying that "It does not require a majority to prevail, but rather an irate, tireless minority keen to set brush fires in people's minds."[316] This has been shown to be true over time–many historians have speculated that only about 30% of the American people supported the American Revolution. Many

---

[315]Jason Ma, *The Blueprint: A Revolutionary Plan to Plant Missional Communities on Campus,* (Bloomington: Baker Publishing Group, 2007)

[316]"Human Kind," Samuel Adams Heritage Society, http://www.samuel-adams-heritage.com/quotes/popular.html

movements rise up in an environment where there are those who support it, those who are opposed to it, and a vast majority who are so wrapped up in their own lives that they do not care either way. This third group is so apathetic that they will go any way the political wind blows. This is why your involvement is so critical. Remember, Thomas Jefferson once said that "We do not have a government of the majority; we have a have a government of the majority who participate."[317]

Do not believe the lie that one man or a small group of people cannot change the course of history for either good or evil. Jesus Christ was one man. The apostle Paul was one man. King David was one man. Moses was one man. Even Hitler was one man. Do not wait for there to be a majority for your cause, or it will never get off the ground. Every forest fire starts with a spark. When that sparked is fanned, the fire spreads very quickly. The same is true with a message and with a cause.

The sacred scripture tells us repeatedly to let our children and our children's children know what the Lord has done. Revival will often break out when God's people hear the testimonies of what He has done in the past and what He is willing to do in the future.

However, whenever a nation abandons the divine authority of Romans 13, they end up on a slippery slope that ultimately results in the acceptance and legalization of ever increasing moral depravity. This *always* ends in a nation's judgment and destruction. God's people must make a choice who they will serve. Either your God will be your King or your king will be your god. You will either hail Caesar, or hail the King of the Jews.

In an article titled: *My Heart Aches for America*, Billy Graham wrote: "Some years ago, my wife, Ruth, was reading the draft of a book I was writing. When she finished a section describing the terrible downward spiral of our nation's moral standards and the idolatry of worshiping false gods such as technology and sex, she startled me by exclaiming, "If God doesn't punish America, He'll

---

[317]"Spurious Quotations," The Jefferson Monticello, https://www.monticello.org/site/research-and-collections/government-majority-who-participate-quotation

have to apologize to Sodom and Gomorrah."[318] He is one of many American leaders who are giving such a warning. Robert H. Bork, Ronald Reagan's nominee for the U.S. Supreme Court, said in his 1996 New York Times bestselling book that we as Americans were "Slouching Towards Gomorrah." This was written before the *Obergefell v. Hodges* decision that legalized homosexual marriage. Today, we are no longer Slouching Towards Gomorrah, we are living in Gomorrah.

For nearly 60 years, this downward slide into despotism and immorality has increased at light speed. It is clear that our politically elected officials at the State, or Federal, level have no intention or political courage to reverse this downward spiral. The Supreme Court has become a den of tyrants. The Court has legalized what God Himself has declared illegal (Abortion, Pornography and Homosexuality) and has criminalized what God Himself has declared our duty, namely praying and teaching God's word to our children.[319] In the appellate court system, we have the right and the authority to Appeal to the next highest court when we feel that a lower court has made an incorrect, illegal, or unconstitutional ruling.

The Christian church has been trying to restrain and reverse the effects that the forces of darkness have had upon this nation, without first understanding the legal actions that are required. Police officers are agents of the state who are responsible for restraining and arresting evil. However, the police must first get legal action in place before they can take action. A judge must issue an arrest warrant prior to most arrests. A judge must issue a search warrant prior to most searches. A judge must issue a restraining or a cease and desist order before police can intervene in many private interactions. Only then can the agents of the state take lawful action against the lawbreakers. Likewise, the people of the Christian church are God's agents on this earth to "loose and to bind", to allow and forbid. However, before we can act as the agents of the Lord, we must first appear before the Supreme Judge in order to

---

318

[319]See 1 Thess 5:17 and Deut.11:18-21

get legal matters in place before we can take action. Even the arch-angel Michael, in contending with Satan over the body of Moses, understood that he first needed the legal authority to act as the Lord's agent.[320]

The only remaining hope is the American people, particularly the Christian church, to make our Appeal to Heaven. In short, by signing on to our "Appealing to Heaven" civil rights movement, we are in fact signing onto a class action lawsuit. We are delivering a heavenly cease and desist order against the forces of darkness and Satan; agents and ministers upon this earth.

In a traditional lawsuit, one party typically sues another party for the redress of a wrong. In these cases, all of the parties are typ-ically present in the court. On the other hand, a class action lawsuit is used when the allegations against the offending party involve a large number of people who have been wronged and/or injured by the same defendant and in the same way. Instead of each injured person bringing their own separate lawsuit, the class action pro-cess allows for all the claims of all class members—whether they know they have been injured or not—to be resolved in a single pro-ceeding. We are confident that when we "Appeal to the Supreme Judge of the Universe" and provide evidence that the kings and the rulers of our nation are breaking His divine law, that we will in fact get a favorable ruling and justice will prevail.

When we truly understand the legal proceedings and ruling that are required before opposing the forces of darkness, we will understand that the Declaration of Independence was, essentially, a class action lawsuit seeking the assistance of heaven to obtain a cease and desist order against the tyrants of Britain. Of the Fifty-six signers of the Declaration of Independence, twenty-five were law-yers and twenty-seven had seminary degrees and understood the procedures for appealing to the Supreme Court of Heaven. Only when Christian ministers, Christian lawyers, and Christian judges once again come together in unity in order to jointly appeal to the Supreme Judge of the universe, will the legal authority be put in place to restrain and subdue that forces of darkness.

---

[320]Jude 8-9 NKJV

The first time Christ came, He came as savior. During the Second Coming, He will be coming as both King and Judge. "Now I saw heaven opened, and behold, a white horse. And He who sat on him was called Faithful and True, and in righteousness He judges and makes war... And He has on His robe and on His thigh a name written: King of Kings and Lord of Lords."[321] It is very possible that our joint "Appeal to Heaven" prayer will be enough to bring about the Second Coming. We are petitioning the Supreme Judge to come and judge the nations. "Even so, come quickly LORD Jesus." The fire that once existed to exult Him as our present day King has left the church leaving us lukewarm to His ruler-ship, both individually and nationally.

Will America be saved or will it fall onto the ash heap of history like every other civilization before us? Only time will tell. If the American church does not do its part in getting their governmental leaders to turn from their wicked way, then as individual Christians we have some tough times ahead. The humanist tendency of man is to simply keep quiet for fear of incurring the wrath of an ungodly world. But Jesus taught "whoever desires to save his life will lose it, but whoever loses his life for My sake will save it."[322]

Do not listen to the words of the prophets and pastors who are waving the white flag to the enemy, and who are willing to capitulate to the kingdom of Satan. Do not listen to those who seduce you into luke-warmness by saying that "Jesus told us this would be one of the signs of the times and that there is nothing you can do about it." Every generation before us thought that it was the terminal generation and for this very reason, luke-warmness has overtaken the people of God, both in the pulpit and at the grassroots level. We must all learn to live by the motto: "Live like He is coming tonight, work like it will be another 1000 years." Jesus *never* taught that we are to throw up the white flag to the gates of hell and "hunker down" in our churches waiting for his return. He told us to "Position yourself" that when He returns, we will be found advancing the kingdom

---

[321]Rev 19:11; 16 NKJV

[322]Luke 9:24 NKJV

of God. Jesus taught: "Blessed is that servant whom his master will find so doing when he comes."[323]

Biblical history shows over and over again that when a nation, or the world, is being prepared judgment for its wickedness, it is only those who did not think of their own life, but rather preached righteousness, who were spared from the wrath to come. During the time of Sodom and Gomorrah, it was only righteous Lot and his family who were spared judgment because he had the courage to rebuke the wicked sodomites.[324] During the time of Noah, it was only righteous Noah and his family that was spared the judgment because he had the courage to preach righteousness.[325]

In a story that is just as relevant today as it was for ancient Israel, at the time of Israel's judgment, it was only those who sighed and cried over all the abominations that were being committed in Israel that were spared from judgment.

> And He called to the man clothed with linen, who had the writer's inkhorn at his side; and the LORD said to him, "Go through the midst of the city, through the midst of Jerusalem, and put a mark on the foreheads of the men who sigh and cry over all the abominations that are done within it." To the others He said in my hearing, "Go after him through the city and kill; do not let your eye spare, nor have any pity. Utterly slay old and young men, maidens and little children and women; but do not come near anyone on whom is the mark; and begin at My sanctuary."[326]

For Israel, judgment began at the house of God because it was God's ministers who had the laws and oracles of God, and should have called the nation to repentance. They refused to be the salt and the light and were the first ones destroyed. The Christian church in

---

[323]Luke 12:43 NKJV

[324]Gen 19:7 NKJV

[325]2 Peter 2:5 NKJV

[326]Ezek 9:3-6 NKJV

America finds itself in the exact same position today. A holy righteous God will not judge the wicked until He has first judged His people. "For the time has come for judgment to begin at the house of God; and if it begins with us first, what will be the end of those who do not obey the gospel of God? Now "If the righteous one is scarcely saved, where will the ungodly and the sinner appear?" Therefore, let those who suffer according to the will of God commit their souls to Him in doing good, as to a faithful Creator.[327]

In Revelation Rev 14:1-5, we once again read about a group of people who will be sealed by a mark on the foreheads. They will be saved from going through the judgments of Revelation because they overcame the fear of man and were willing to sigh and cry over all the abominations that were done.[328]

As we saw in the opening of the book, the historical cycle of world civilizations proves that it is only faith and courage that ever leads a nation back to freedom and liberty. I will leave you with a quote from former U.S. Senator Zell Miller (D–GA) as he stood on the Senate floor on Feb 12, 2004, and said the following:

> "Arnold Toynbee, who wrote the acclaimed 12-volume A Study of History, once declared, 'Of the 22 civilizations that have appeared in history, 19 of them collapsed when they reached the moral state America is in today. Toynbee died in 1975, before seeing the worst that was yet to come. Yes, Arnold Toynbee saw the famine. The 'famine of hearing the words of the Lord.' Whether it is removing a display of the Ten Commandments from a courthouse or the Nativity scene from a city square. Whether it is eliminating prayer in schools or eliminating 'under God' in the Pledge of Allegiance. Whether it is making a mockery of the sacred institution of marriage between a man and woman or, yes, telecasting

---

[327]1 Peter 4:17-19 NKJV

[328]See Rev 3

around the world made-in-the-USA filth masquerading as entertainment...

"Everyone today seems to think that the U.S. Constitution expressly provides for separation of church and state. Ask any ten people if that's not so. And I'll bet you most of them will say 'Well, sure.' And some will point out, 'It's in the First Amendment.' "Wrong! Read it! It says, 'Congress shall make no law respecting an establishment of religion or prohibiting the free exercise thereof.' Where is the word 'separate'? Where are the words 'church' or 'state?'

"They are not there. Never have been. Never intended to be. Read the Congressional Records during that four-month period in 1789 when the amendment was being framed in Congress. Clearly their intent was to prohibit a single denomination in exclusion of all others, whether it was Anglican or Catholic or some other."

I highly recommend a great book entitled Original Intent by David Barton. It really gets into how the actual members of Congress, who drafted the First Amendment, expected basic biblical principles and values to be present throughout public life and society, not separate from it.

"It was Alexander Hamilton who pointed out that 'judges should be bound down by strict rules and precedents, which serve to define and point out their duty.' Bound down! That is exactly what is needed to be done. There was not a single precedent cited when school prayer was struck down in 1962." These judges who legislate instead of adjudicate, do it without being responsible to one single solitary voter for their actions. Among the signers of the Declaration of Independence was a brilliant young physician from Pennsylvania named Benjamin Rush. When Rush was elected to that First Continental Congress, his close friend Benjamin Franklin told him, 'We need you.... we have a great task before us, assigned to us by Providence.'

"Today, 228 years later, there is still a great task before us assigned to us by Providence. Our founding fathers did not shirk their duty and we can do no less. "By the way, Benjamin Rush was once asked a question that has long interested this senator from Georgia in particular. Dr. Rush was asked, are you a democrat or an aristocrat? And the good doctor answered, 'I am neither. I am a Christocrat. I believe He, alone, who created and redeemed man is qualified to govern him.' That reply of Benjamin Rush is just as true today in the year of our Lord 2016 as it was in the year of our Lord 1776.

"So, if I am asked why, with all the pressing problems this nation faces today, why am I pushing these social issues and taking the Senate's valuable time? I will answer: Because, it is of the highest importance. Yes, there's a deficit to be concerned about in this country, a deficit of decency. "So, as the sand empties through my hourglass at warp speed, and with my time running out in this Senate and on this earth, I feel compelled to speak out. For I truly believe that at times like this, silence is not golden. It is yellow."[329]

---

[329]David Barton, *Original Intent: The Courts, the Constitution, and Religion*, (Wallbuilders, 2008)

It is time to quit being good Republicans and good Democrats and start being good Americans. A good American used to be a Christocrat! As Americans, we used to be "one nation under God", but now we are on the precipice of being a nation gone under. As Americans, we used to believe in the divine chain of command, expressed in Romans 13, that teaches us that He alone, who created and redeemed man, is qualified to govern him. As Abraham Lincoln reminded America, "we have forgotten God. We have forgotten the gracious hand which preserved us in peace, and multiplied and enriched and strengthened us; and we have vainly imagined, in the deceitfulness of our hearts, that all these blessings were produced by some superior wisdom and virtue of our own. Intoxicated with unbroken success, we have become too self-sufficient to feel the necessity of redeeming and preserving grace, too proud to pray to the God that made us!"[330]

God, in his mercy, has been warning America in the exact same way that He warned ancient Israel before it was judged. Jonathan Cahn, President of Hope of the World ministries and author of the best-selling book *The Harbingers,* produced a video titled The Isaiah 9:10 Judgment. I can testify that this video changed our church! I would *highly* recommend mass viewing parties of this video in every church and in every available venue across America.

Recently, men of faith, such as Dutch Sheets, Lou Engel, and Lewis Hogan have started national prayer movements that gather together people who are willing to "sigh and cry over all the abomi-nations" that are being committed in America. Dran Reese, President of The Salt & Light Council (SLC), has established a ministry that trains and equips churches to start Salt & Light Biblical Citizenship Ministries. SLC provides a turn-key program for activating the Church to become a positive influence and witness for our Judeo-Christian values in the public sector. This includes arming churches nationwide with strategic prayer initiatives, Bible-centric education that addresses pressing national issues, effective and sustainable action, and legal backing.

---

[330]Abraham Lincoln, "Proclamation Appointing a National Fast Day," (Speech: Washington, DC, March 30, 1863) Abraham Lincoln Online, http://www. abrahamlincolnonline.org/lincoln/speeches/fast.htm

Are you someone who will include yourself among the ranks of those who will Appeal to Heaven, and begin "sighing and crying over all the abominations" that are being committed in America? Are you one of the many who sit idly by while all these abominations are being committed all around you? Remember, Jesus told us that "You are the salt of the earth; but if the salt loses its flavor, how shall it be seasoned? It is then good for nothing but to be thrown out and trampled underfoot by men." Lot's wife was turned into a pillar of salt because she loved the wickedness of Sodom and looked back when she was clearly warned not to. What a tragic testimony when she was turned in her death what she never was in her life. "Remember Lot's wife."[331] Therefore, I leave you with the following charge:

> I solemnly charge you in the presence of God and of Christ Jesus, who is to judge the living and the dead, and by His appearing and His kingdom: preach the word; be ready in season and out of season; reprove, rebuke, exhort, with great patience and instruction. For the time will come when they will not endure sound doctrine; but wanting to have their ears tickled, they will accumulate for themselves teachers in accordance to their own desires, and will turn away their ears from the truth and will turn aside to myths. But you, be sober in all things, endure hardship, do the work of an evangelist, fulfill your ministry.[332]

~ 2 Timothy 4:1-5

---

[331]Luke 17:32 NKJV

[332]2 Tim 4:1-5 NKJV

Action Items

Many people who hear this message want to know what they can do to promote the restoration of our Christian- based Constitutional Republic. We understand that most Americans do not have a lot of time or the money at their disposal. Therefore, our marketing and strategy teams have developed a list of "Action Items" that nearly every person can implement, in order to be a part of the national grassroots movement. These items are as follows:

1. PRAY – The most important action item is prayer. That might sound simplistic, but it is the foundation for the entire movement. This nation cannot be delivered from the hands of our enemies unless we *"Appeal to the Supreme Judge of the universe for the righteousness of our intentions."* We must understand the legal, and judicial, principle that a judge cannot act unless someone comes before his court as a petitioner. You can either use the Appeal to Heaven prayer found in this book or downloading the "We are Appealing to Heaven" app from our website at http://appealingtoheaven.org/, or from the iTunes store.

2. RAISE AWARENESS – We must also raise awareness that our God-given and constitutionally protected rights are being violated. The most important way to help with this campaign, is to display our "We are Appealing to Heaven" awareness items. Every influential movement has had a flag to symbolize

it agenda. Most recently, this was used very effectively by the LGBT community. The creator of the "Gay Rights" rainbow flag, Gilbert Baker, spoke of its importance:

"The flag is an action – it's more than just the cloth and the stripes. When a person puts the Rainbow Flag on his car or his house, they're not just flying a flag. They're taking action."

By flying an Appeal to Heaven flag over your churches, homes, and businesses, you are taking an action to raise awareness of our cause for religious freedom, liberty, and the restoration of our Christian-based Constitutional Republic. If you do not have a place to display an Appeal to Heaven flag, you can still use one of our other action items. We have created numerous "We are Appealing to Heaven" aware-ness items that will help. These include yard signs, magnets, bumper stickers, and more! The more that people begin to see these items, the more it will raise their curiosity. This will give us the opportunity to educate on the foundations of the American Republic.

3. EDUCATE – Our Appeal to Heaven book, and the accom-panying Teachers Study Guide, was created in order to edu-cate patriotic Christian Americans about the true historical foundations of our nation. All the institutions that should be teaching these truths have been turned against us. The government controlled media, public schools, and univer-sities will be no help. Therefore, the Christian church is the only institution left in America that has a network powerful enough to start and sustain such a movement. The book was created to be used like Rick Warren's *The Purpose Driven Life*. Start a Salt and Light Council Ministry in your local Church. The Salt & Light Council (SLC), has been estab-lished in order to train and equip churches to start Salt & Light Biblical Citizenship Ministries. SLC provides a turnkey program for activating the Church to become a positive influ-ence and witness for our Judeo-Christian values in the public

sector. This includes arming churches nationwide with strategic prayer initiatives, Bible-centric education that addresses pressing national issues, effective and sustainable action, and legal backing. You can contact them at https://saltandlight-council.org/contact/ for more information.

4. SPREAD OUR MESSAGE THROUGH SOCIAL MEDIA – As was already stated, the biased media, public schools, and universities primarily determine the information that the public receives. However, the use of social media is quickly becoming the "Gutenberg Press" of our day. This is why the government is trying to restrict control of the internet by labeling many Christian, and other patriotic sites, as "Fake News." Any restriction of our freedom of religion, freedom of speech, and freedom of the press is a violation of constitutional law, and therefore illegal. We may not always agree with each other, but we should fight for each other's right to speak freely. Only un-American, totalitarian governments seek to use tyranny as a means to suppress our God-given and constitutionally protected rights.

5. DONATE – Presently, we do not have the resources to fund a "National Civil Rights Campaign," to include conferences and speaking tours. President Obama was able to raise four million dollars in a 24-hour period, with just 130,000 people giving an average of $23 each. I believe that the Christian Church can do much better. Your donation to Peacemakers Outreach is also tax-deductible.

Check our website, www.appealingtoheaven.org, in order donate and find up-to-date ways to engage.